# Introduction to Knowledge Management: KM in Business

# Introduction to Knowledge Management: KM in Business

*Todd R. Groff and Thomas P. Jones*

*An Imprint of Elsevier*

Amsterdam   Boston   London   New York   Oxford   Paris   San Diego
San Francisco   Singapore   Sydney   Tokyo

Butterworth–Heinemann

*An Imprint of Elsevier*

♾Recognizing the importance of preserving what has been written, Elsevier Science prints its books on acid-free paper whenever possible.

**Library of Congress Cataloging-in-Publication Data**

Groff, Todd R.
    Introduction to knowledge management: KM in business/Todd R. Groff and Thomas
P. Jones.
      p. cm.
    Includes bibliographical references and index.
    ISBN 0-7506-7728-7 (pbk. : alk. paper)
      1. Knowledge management. I. Jones, Thomas P. II. Title.

HD30.2.G76 2003
658.4′038—dc21
                                          2003043696

**British Library Cataloguing-in-Publication Data**

A catalogue record for this book is available from the British Library.

The publisher offers special discounts on bulk orders of this book.
For information, please contact:

Manager of Special Sales
Elsevier
200 Wheeler Road
Burlington, MA 01803
Tel: 781-313-4700
Fax: 781-313-4882

For information on all Butterworth–Heinemann publications available, contact our World Wide Web home page at: http://www.bh.com

10 9 8 7 6 5 4 3 2

Printed in the United States of America

# Contents

# Introducing KM

*An immense and ever-increasing wealth of knowledge is scattered about the world today; knowledge that would probably suffice to solve all the mighty difficulties of our age, but it is dispersed and unorganized. We need a sort of mental clearing house for the mind: a depot where knowledge and ideas are received, sorted, summarized, digested, clarified and compared.*

—H.G. Wells in *The Brain: Organization of the Modern World,* 1940

**Chapter One Learning Objectives**

- ❑ Learn why knowledge is considered the "Infinite Asset."
- ❑ See the key differences between data, information, and knowledge.
- ❑ Learn to recognize both tacit and explicit knowledge.
- ❑ Begin exploring the concept of "scope creep."

Faster, better, cheaper—this is the call of the wild for business in today's rapidly changing market. Each new class of eager young students graduating from our schools shows up more computer literate and Web savvy than the class before it, only to find their costly training becoming obsolete at a frightening pace. Workers entering the job market today had better be armed with the latest tools, techniques, strategies, and information resources if they hope to succeed. For those hoping to start a small business, the need is even greater.

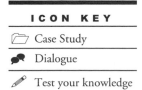

**ICON KEY**

📁 Case Study

🐛 Dialogue

✏ Test your knowledge

**To prepare you for this hostile, fast-paced environment,** we have put together our comprehensive knowledge management (KM) study as a series of explanations, demonstrations, and practical applications. We hope these concepts will help you effectively harness the infinite asset of shared knowledge.

## How to Use This Book

The icon key describes how each section will be annotated to allow you to quickly navigate to the section of the text that you are looking for.

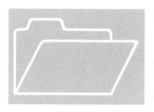

### About the Case Studies

Case studies are taken from real-world businesses struggling daily to re-create themselves for success in the information economy. They are intended to provide students with an understanding of how KM practices can drastically impact the bottom line of any business.

## What Is Knowledge Management?

**The Infinite Asset**
Knowledge is often called the *infinite asset* because it is the only asset that increases when it is shared.

In recent years, the meaning of the term *knowledge management* (KM) has been debated, defined, and redefined repeatedly. In our book, KM is taken as **the tools, techniques, and strategies to retain, analyze, organize, improve, and share business expertise**. Traditional businesses have aimed to ensure success based primarily on the management of finite physical resources. Now, information economy companies pursue rapid innovation, business agility, and just-in-time learning. They hope to develop and retain their "infinite assets," the knowledge of their people. Unlike most assets, knowledge is not depleted when it is shared. In fact, sharing knowledge almost invariably results in increased knowledge for both parties.

It has been argued that *knowledge management* is a poor term because knowledge cannot be managed. This is because knowledge lives primarily in the mind. *Information management* doesn't prove to be much of an improvement in terminology because it carries with it decades of baggage and preconceptions that focus solely on technology. Effective management of your infinite assets requires a much broader focus that includes the philosophies, techniques, and infrastructure components necessary to drive collaboration, innovation, and business agility. KM focuses on utilizing new ways to channel raw data into meaningful information—and hopefully knowledge.

**Knowledge is NOT simply information.** Knowledge resides in the users of information, not the containers. Several key factors distinguish among knowledge, information, and data. Understanding the differences is central to effectively leveraging them.

## Data, Information, and Knowledge

**Data:** The nature of data is raw and without context. It simply exists and has no significance beyond its existence. It can exist in any form, usable or not. A spreadsheet generally starts out by holding data, such as a list of dollar figures.

**Information:** Information is data that have been given meaning by way of context. A spreadsheet is often used to make information from the data stored within it. A good example would be an income statement for your business. It is still a list of dollar figures, but now it has a relevant context.

**Knowledge:** Knowledge is information combined with understanding and capability; it lives in the minds of people. Typically, knowledge provides a level of predictability that usually stems from the recognition of patterns. The astute executive *knows* the significance of the dollar figures on his or her company's income statement, and this makes him or her capable of taking positive action. Knowledge guides action, whereas information and data can merely inform or confuse.

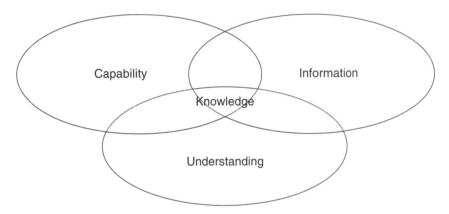

FIGURE 1.1  Venn diagram shows the relationship between information and knowledge.

**There are two main types of knowledge;** the first and most common type of knowledge is called **tacit knowledge**. The second type is called **explicit knowledge**.

**Tacit knowledge** refers to personal knowledge embedded in individual experience and involving intangible factors such as personal belief, perspective, and values. Tacit knowledge can be extremely difficult to transfer. This is a point that any parent should recognize immediately. If you have ever tried to teach your child something as seemingly simple as how to properly hold a pencil, you have realized that many things that are easy for you to do are almost impossible for you to explain.

**Explicit knowledge** refers to tacit knowledge that has been documented. It has been articulated into formal language and can be much more easily transferred among individuals. Making tacit knowledge explicit is one of the key functions of a KM strategy.

## Knowledgebases

Many organizations are now implementing **knowledgebases** as a strategy for making more of their employees' tacit knowledge explicit. Knowledgebases are digital databases that attempt to capture almost every imaginable explicit intellectual asset that an organization possesses. They can provide a rich source of research material for problem solving, a powerful archive for organizational best practices, and a shared forum for competitive intelligence.

## Constructing Knowledgebases

Knowledgebase construction entails the capture, processing, storage, delivery, and maintenance of huge amounts of information about products, people, processes, and policies. Much of this content doesn't exist at the beginning of the KM initiative. It has to be created from scratch as relevant facts are discovered. What does exist in the beginning always comes from diverse sources, in diverse formats.

> **Note:**
>
> Details on constructing a knowledgebase for yourself or your workgroup will be covered in a later chapter in this text.

**Dialogue**

What types of tacit knowledge do you think would be valuable to capture into a corporate knowledgebase?

What benefits for the company do you imagine could be gained from making this knowledge explicit?

# Making Tacit Knowledge Explicit

Interview one member of your family, class, or immediate circle of friends. Ask them to describe three of their favorite ways to save money. Next, create a document describing the three methods so that a third party could repeat them from the written documentation alone.

1. **Create a list of three money-saving techniques.** Try to choose novel or unexpected methods. They may be harder to document, but they are almost always more valuable.

2. **Document the exact procedures involved.** Documenting an individual's processes can be quite challenging. Avoid making the procedure so specific that it doesn't apply to a diverse group of individuals. For example, driving to 7-Eleven to buy bread instead of QuikTrip because it is closer to your home.

# Making Explicit Knowledge Retrievable

It is simply not enough to pile all of your electronic files into a folder on a shared drive and call that a knowledgebase. Like any records management system, for a knowledgebase to be effective, the documents contained in the knowledgebase must be easily retrievable, saved in a commonly accessible format, and fully keyword searchable. To make this happen, there are three critical technical components: the user interface, the index fields, and the taxonomy, which must be planned out carefully.

**User Interface:** The combination of menus, screen design, keyboard commands, command language, and online help, which creates the way a user interacts with a computer. This is important because a poor user interface to your knowledgebase almost assures the eventual lack of acceptance by the intended end users.

**Index Fields:** Also known as **metadata**, the index fields in a record hold the *unique* data that identifies that record from all of the other records in the file or database. File Type, Location, Description, and Author Name are typical index fields. Indexes are defined using very specific data types such as Date Fields, Currency Fields, Number Fields, and Text Fields. Choosing the wrong data type for a property in your index can make your information difficult or impossible to retrieve.

**Taxonomy:** The rules and principles used to ensure consistent classification of data into ordered categories. For example, taxonomy rules might determine whether you save your recently created security procedures document into the Security category or the Documentation category of your knowledgebase.

When it comes to ease of use and customer acceptance of a knowledgebase, the user interface is where the rubber meets the road. In order to be effective, a knowledgebase user interface (UI) must provide the strict enforcement of your taxonomy rules, easy publishing, easy searching, and rapid summary review of the search results that are returned.

The publishing process includes uploading the user's document into the system and then allowing the user to enter data for the key index fields. Easy publishing is a must because getting people to author to the knowledgebase is one of the toughest KM challenges you will face. Typical employees who are not trained in KM view authoring to a public knowledgebase as too risky to try without a clearly visible incentive. The drive to increase authoring to the knowledgebase will be difficult enough without having to force users to accept a complicated and/or time-consuming data entry process.

Developing your set of rules for consistent classification of data—your taxonomy—can be one of the most difficult parts of creating a knowledgebase. Date formats must be consistent if users are going to look up documents by date. Categories must be clearly understandable, unambiguous, and mutually exclusive. Most important, the taxonomy must support the objectives defined in the scope of the project. Later in this book, you will have an opportunity to devise your own taxonomy to support a shared workgroup knowledgebase.

Making tacit knowledge explicit is a valuable and difficult activity. Ensuring easy retrieval of these hard-won intellectual assets is far too critical to approach without clear planning. Often, the best place to begin is with your project documentation.

# Project Planning

All failed projects share one key problem: the failure to meet customer expectations. The cause is poor project planning and management. In this section, we will show you some ways to meet your customers' expectations—the most important goal for anyone in business. You cannot possibly give your customers everything that they want, and you probably cannot get them to take everything they need, so the best course of action lies in effectively setting the customers' expectations. A common tool for setting customer expectations is the scope document.

# The Scope Document

The scope document defines the objectives, timeframe, assumptions, and limitations inherent in your project. It provides a context in which to discuss the resources, functionality, stakeholders, and schedule of the project. It also seeks to clarify, codify, and make explicit the customers' tacit expectations. By looking at the objectives early in the project, it gives the project manager a way of controlling **scope creep**, as well as improving customer buy-in.

**Scope Creep:** A phrase used to describe a situation in which project goals are altered or expanded so often that the assignment no longer resembles the original project commitment.

**Scope Document:** A document that gets the customer to sign off on the objectives, timeframe, assumptions, limitations, stakeholders, risks, and responsibilities in a project before beginning work.

FIGURE 1.2 **Scope Triangle.** Shows the relationship between time, functionality, and cost.

The scope document typically evolves as the project continues and more is learned. It is important to realize that working to avoiding scope creep does not mean that the scope of the project is unchangeable. Project management is a dynamic process that is not limited to technical models and methodologies but is linked to important and evolving organizational, political, cultural, and business issues; however, customers have a tendency to focus on three points: cost, functionality, and implementation time. Typically, these three points are thought of as sides of a triangle. Altering any one side of the triangle forces you to change the other two sides and as a result changes the triangle's overall size and area.

### Case Study: Scope Creep

In 1997, ABC Company decided to implement an enterprise resource planning (ERP) system. Spanning "the complete supply-chain life cycle," the ERP system would pull together the company's financial reporting, planning, procurement, production, inventory control, and bill-paying functions. Senior management believed this system would save money by eliminating duplication of effort and raise profits by consolidating key strategic information.

| SCOPE | Project Name: | Project By: | Requested By: |
|---|---|---|---|
| **Problem/Opportunity:** | | | |
| **Goal:** | | | |
| **Objectives:** | | | |
| **Success Criteria:** | | | |
| **Assumptions, Risks, Obstacles:** | | | |
| **Stakeholders:** | | **Projected Timeframe:** | |
| **Author:** | **Date:** | **Approved By:** | **Dept:** |

FIGURE 1.3 Sample format for a simple scope document.

After ABC Company officially kicked off its installation of a PeopleSoft ERP system in March 1998, members of its finance, sales, marketing, and other departments signed off on the reports and functions they would require. The director in charge of delivering the project met with the technical team and arrived at an estimate of the costs and time required to implement the goals. At that point, the plan was presented to the senior management, who gave their approval to begin work. The total ERP package, including hardware, software, and consulting, was estimated to cost the company $2 million and take two years to complete.

Then the business environment changed. ABC Company merged with DES Industries in August 1998. Management did not believe this situation would be a large problem for the ERP implementation because DES Industries was already using PeopleSoft. They would simply need to **expand the scope** of the project to include integrating the existing DES PeopleSoft system with the new one ABC Company was purchasing.

Good project planning would now require that the cost and timeframe estimates for the project be reassessed to meet the new objective, but, as with any company merger, the influx of new management personnel created the need to reassign various employees from both original organizations to new positions. One of the employees moved was the technical manager in charge of the PeopleSoft project. As a result, the **cost and timeframe estimates were not reassessed**.

It wasn't long before it became obvious that the project was not going to be delivered either on time or on budget. That's when things got ugly. Managers from the various functional areas quickly began trying to distance themselves from the project and attempting to assign blame for the failure. A newly appointed vice president then made a commitment to the top-level corporate management to have the project completed in a timeframe that was even shorter than the original estimate.

In the end, the project came in **two years late and 200% over budget**. The director in charge of the project lost his position with the company, and the amount of bitterness and internal fighting within the company increased by an order of magnitude. The users, having seen so few of their expectations met, still believe that the software package is deeply flawed and long for the "good old days" of disconnected systems and massive redundancy.

### Additional Learning Resources

- ❑ www.yourdoorway.to/classifying-information-and-data—An open portal designed to provide access to a variety of information classification resources
- ❑ *Modern Project Management: Successfully Integrating Project Management Knowledge Areas and Processes,* by Norman R. Howes
- ❑ www.brint.com—KM portal for business, information, technology, and knowledge management for professionals and entrepreneurs
- ❑ www.intelligentkm.com—Magazine devoted to knowledge management and its role in the extended, intelligent enterprise

 **Test Your Knowledge**

## Discussion Questions

1. In your opinion, where is knowledge created?

2. In your opinion, what tools do workers entering the job market need?

3. What have traditional businesses primarily used to ensure success?

4. What do information economy companies pursue?

5.  Where does knowledge primarily reside? Why?

6.  What does knowledge management focus on?

7.  What are the two main types of knowledge?

8.  Why are companies now implementing knowledgebases?

## Review Questions

1. It has been argued that _____ _____ is a poor term because knowledge cannot be managed.

2. Effective management of your infinite assets requires a much broader focus that includes the _____, _____, and _____ components necessary to drive collaboration, innovation, and business agility.

3. Knowledge resides in the _____ of information, not the containers.

4. Knowledgebases are _____ _____ of every imaginable explicit corporate intellectual asset.

5. They provide a rich source of research material for _____, a powerful archive for organizational _____, and a shared forum for competitive intelligence.

6. Like any records management system, for a knowledgebase to be effective, the _____ contained in the knowledgebase must be easily _____, saved in a commonly accessible format, and fully _____ searchable.

7. User interface (UI) must provide the strict enforcement of your _____ _____, easy publishing, easy searching, and rapid summary review of the search results that are returned.

8. Project management is a _____ _____ that is not limited to technical models and methodologies but is linked to important and evolving organizational, political, cultural, and business issues.

9. Typical employees who are not trained in KM view _____ to a public knowledgebase as too risky to try without a clearly visible incentive.

10. Most important, the _____ must support the objectives defined in the scope of the project.

## Chapter Vocabulary

**Data:** Raw facts and figures, such as orders and payments, which are processed into information, such as balance due and quantity on hand.

**Explicit knowledge:** Knowledge that has been documented or articulated into formal language in order to be more easily transferred among individuals.

**Index fields:** See also *metadata*.

**Infinite asset:** The knowledge possessed by the employees of a corporation.

**Information:** Information is the summarization of data; it has been given meaning by way of context.

**Knowledge:** Information combined with understanding and capability, living in the minds of people.

**Knowledge management:** The tools, techniques, and strategies to retain, analyze, organize, and share business expertise.

**Knowledgebase:** Digital database of explicit corporate intellectual assets.

**Metadata:** Fields in a record holding the unique data that identifies a unique record from all of the other records in the file or database.

**Retrievable:** Capable of being regained, especially with effort.

**Scope creep:** A phrase used to describe a situation in which project goals are altered or expanded so often that the assignment no longer resembles the original project commitment.

**Scope document:** A document that gets the customer to sign off on the objectives, timeframe, assumptions, limitations, stakeholders, risks, and responsibilities in a project before beginning work.

**Tacit knowledge:** Personal knowledge embedded in individual experience and involving intangible factors such as personal belief, perspective, and values.

**Taxonomy:** A set of rules and principles to ensure consistent classification of data into ordered categories.

**User interface:** The combination of menus, screen design, keyboard commands, command language, and online help, which creates the way a user interacts with a computer.

# Personal KM

*The Romans were a very ingenious culture; they incorporated engineering into all facets of their culture. The roads they built allowed their armies to quickly move from one end of their empire to the other. Our interstate highway system was built for the same reason. Their highway system also increased commerce throughout their empire, providing two-fold benefits for their construction. The Romans invented aqueducts to move water, concrete to strengthen building construction, and indoor plumbing, but still their empire fell.*

*The steam engine was first discovered and documented by the Romans, but Caesar was required to bless all ideas before they could receive any creditability or funding. Caesar never approved the steam engine, and therefore it was shelved for another millennium and a half. Innovation must be allowed to grow within an organization, or that organization will lose its competitive edge.*

### Chapter Two Learning Objectives
- ❑ Recognize that the presentation of information can either hide or highlight the truth.
- ❑ Learn to value the path to knowledge, as much as the knowledge itself.
- ❑ Know what determines the utility of a network.
- ❑ Learn the six most common tools for personal KM.

## Thoughts on KM

Traditionally, leader-driven plans and goals—aimed to ensure optimization and efficiencies based primarily on consensus, compliance, and the management of finite physical resources—have driven businesses. Today, cutting-edge companies pursue open dialogue, rapid innovation, and business agility by developing their infinite assets—the knowledge of their people. Yogesh Malhotra, in Knowledge Assets in the Global Economy, put it like this: "In contrast to the traditional factors of production that were governed by diminishing returns, every additional unit of knowledge used effectively results in a marginal increase in performance."

All business processes involve creation, dissemination, renewal, and application of knowledge toward meeting the goals of the business. Unfortunately, all business processes also involve the hoarding, distorting, and dissemination of disinformation to support the goals of individual employees.

It is critical to avoid focusing on gadgetry while disregarding how people in organizations actually go about acquiring, sharing, and creating new knowledge. After all, most knowledge currently being exchanged in companies is transferred in that most analog of medias—the face-to-face conversation.

> *Successful knowledge transfer involves neither computers nor documents but rather interactions between people.*
>
> —Thomas H. Davenport, "Think Tank: The Future of Knowledge Management," *CIO*, December 15, 1995

In 1971, C.W. Churchman realized that knowledge lives within people, not within databases. His book, *The Design of INQUIRING SYSTEMS: Basic Concepts of Systems and Organization*, provided a wealth of insights into KM long before the beginning of the KM fad. People transform information and data into knowledge by applying context and judgment. The application of context and judgment to information is not a logical target for automation. For this difficult task, culture has traditionally been the tool of choice. Developing a culture of KM involves tasks such as encouraging trust building, collaboration, connectivity, and dynamic communication paths.

KM seeks to develop a strategy that helps spread the expertise of individuals or groups across organizations in ways that directly affect the bottom line. It seeks to establish forums where best practices are shared, defined, refined, debunked, or disseminated. Best practices can only be best if they are continually reviewed and revitalized because today's best practice can often become tomorrow's worst nightmare.

Many companies are now asking their IT organizations to explore knowledge management because they've heard that KM is the next big competitive advantage. Too often, however, the typical IT department's first reaction is to evaluate, buy, install, or even build multimillion-dollar KM technologies and then wait for the business to be transformed. Sadly, it just isn't that easy. Much like the current crisis in voter participation, it is a three-pronged issue: There is a technological component and a procedural component, but by far the biggest barrier is cultural.

### Dialogue

How did Native Americans transfer knowledge before their written language?

How was their knowledge transfer tied to their culture?

# Getting Started without a Corporate KM Initiative

Not all organizations have embraced KM as a vital link to their success, and this can cause some difficulties getting started. Other organizations have realized the importance of KM but are still years away from implementing a solution that filters down to the tactical level. If you are convinced of the importance of KM, don't wait for your company to take the lead. A great way to get started is to look within your own organization, find where KM is already happening, and get involved.

If KM does not already exist in your organization, or if you just want to experiment in KM, then try personal KM. The concepts work basically the same, and it is a good opportunity to get your feet wet. Personal KM should be approached with a formal plan documenting what you hope to achieve and what your expectations are. This document can be the first to be placed in your knowledgebase. Later you can refer back to the document as a measure of how successful you have been.

# Planning Your Personal Knowledgebase

As we get started, remember the following five personal KM tools to be used during this exercise: (1) relevant metrics, (2) system analysis techniques, (3) peer network/dialogue forum, (4) information retrieval tool, and (5) presentation techniques.

### Relevant Metrics

It has been said many times that "if you can't measure it, you can't manage it." To clearly and accurately assess tactical situations, you must be as fully aware of the situation as possible. An accomplished carpenter might phrase it like this: "The key is to measure twice and cut once."

### System Analysis Techniques

Once you have collected as much information as possible about a situation, it is time to begin the system analysis. Any system is made up of inputs, outputs, processes, resources, and objectives. The more completely you identify these components, the better your ability to apply leverage will be, and leverage is how small people make big things happen.

### Peer Network/Dialogue Forum

**Catalyst**

cat·a·lyst
n.
Chemistry. A substance, usually used in small amounts relative to the reactants, that modifies and increases the rate of a reaction without being consumed in the process.

An open and vibrant peer network and dialogue forum is your best bet for driving forward innovation. It is the catalyst. Some of the biggest innovations that science has achieved in the last century are directly the result of smart people kicking around ideas over lunch. Personal insight and current relevance are key differences between information and knowledge. Your peer network/dialogue forum is the best tool in your arsenal to help provide both a source of informational metrics as well as insight and relevance.

## Information Retrieval Tools

Many tools can help you retrieve critical information when you need it. As a knowledge worker, it is imperative that you stay on the forefront of this technology. Portals, search engines, databases, and newsgroups represent a small portion of the tools that are available.

## Presentation Techniques

Innovations that are not accurately, eloquently, and effectively presented are rarely implemented. The techniques you use to deliver your ideas to key decision makers can be the difference between success and failure—no matter how good your idea is.

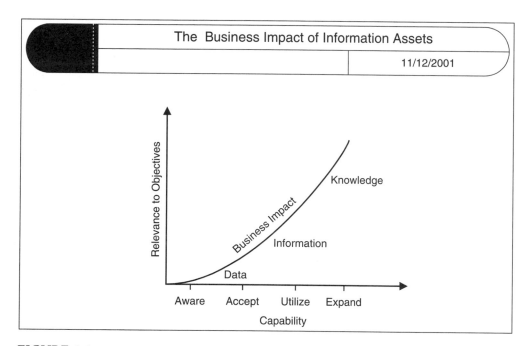

FIGURE 2.1 **Information Assets Impact.** Demonstrates the business impact of information assets in relation to the business objectives.

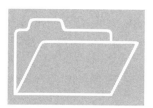

### Case Study: London Cholera Epidemic of 1854

Edward R. Tufte has become one of history's key thought leaders in the visual assessment of data. His three classic books on information design (*The Visual Display of Quantitative Information, Envisioning Information,* and *Visual Explanations*) provide a wealth of advice and techniques for bringing data to life and drawing out the information that makes it valuable. *Visual Explanations* (Cheshire, CT:

Graphics Press, 1997) provides one of history's most compelling cases for using the techniques you will learn in this book. This case was the London Cholera Epidemic of 1854.

The dreaded disease of cholera broke out in central London on August 31, 1854. Within a 250-yard perimeter, there were more than 500 fatal cholera attacks in just 10 days. The number would have been even higher, had it not been for the desperate flight of a large portion of the area's citizens. John Snow's experiences investigating other epidemics led him to believe that the cause was contaminated water, but his testing seemed to show no suspicious impurities; however, as it has often been said, absence of evidence is not the same as evidence of absence.

As the death certificates piled up, the need for immediate action became clearer and clearer. Taking a look at the existing data collected, Snow was shown the data as a date-ordered series of deaths. This provided little more than a scorecard account of the tragedy. Obviously, the objective of the research was to find causality. Although the amount of data available (i.e., death certificates) was increasing by the hour, Snow desperately needed more information. Often, new information can be obtained by changing the presentation of data, and this is just what he did.

By taking the information from the death certificates and changing the plotting of it, John Snow found the cause of the epidemic and a fundamental solution to the problem. Taking a map of the local area, Snow marked the locations of the community's 13 water wells, then plotted the deaths by location. The resulting map revealed a chilling correlation between cholera deaths and proximity to a water pump at the corner of Cambridge and Broad Streets. Meeting with the town's leaders, John Snow advocated the immediate removal of the handle from the Broad Street pump. Although none of the town's leaders was willing to believe that this was the cause of the epidemic, they did have the good sense to give it a try. The epidemic soon ended.

John Snow had demonstrated that cholera was transmitted through water (not air, as many believed at the time) and single-handedly changed the course of modern epidemiology.

## What Are the Lessons of This Story?
- ❑ To draw valuable information from data, it must be presented in the appropriate context.
- ❑ Don't mistake common assumptions for common knowledge. When the knowledge you have gained through your experiences provides you with a hunch, use it, because true knowledge is rarely common and is always improved by more investigation.
- ❑ Build your arsenal of analysis and data visualization tools.
- ❑ Often, new information can be obtained by changing the presentation of the data.

## Organizing Your Information

> *If I have seen further it is by standing on the shoulders of giants.*
> —Sir Isaac Newton
>
> *I use not only the brains I have, but all that I can borrow.*
> —Woodrow Wilson

The goal of your personal KM strategy is simple: to increase your productivity, innovation, and creative output in order to outdistance the competition. Although your personal KM plans will be different depending on your needs and role within the organization, you will need to focus on certain elements to create a workable plan. Develop these elements well, and you will have a personal KM strategy that will improve your ability to deliver solutions, recognize changing market trends, and increase your recognition within the company.

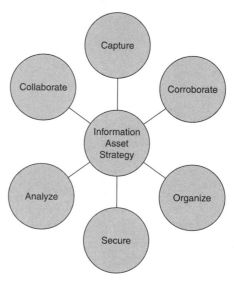

## Six Action Elements of Your Info Workflow

FIGURE 2.2 **Six Action Elements.**

No matter what type of information resources you are managing, you should plan to focus on the following six key actions: capture, corroborate, organize, secure, analyze, and collaborate. In this chapter, we will briefly discuss each action.

## Capture

The capture process provides your system with the actual information and data that you have deemed worthy of inclusion in your system. The capture process may be the most important action element in your personal information workflow. By setting up an aggressive data/information capture process, you can keep yourself informed with the latest news and updates in a myriad of categories without building mountains of irretrievable information.

❑ Set up a wide variety of sources for information and data that can be easily sorted through and prioritized.

❑ Use automated sorting, filtering, and summarizing tools to quickly separate the wheat from the chaff.

❑ Capture information to a flexible, widely used document format that will retain the integrity of the information. **Remember:** A document is no longer just a piece of paper. It can be a Web page, an e-mail message, or a row from a database.

For electronic documents that you personally create, you will want to capture not just the information within a document but also the steps in its creation. For this reason, it is suggested that you consider every document as a potential template.

### Every Document Is a Template

One key recurring theme of KM is the preference for digital vs. analog information. One of the many reasons for this preference is the ease of creating templates. Every time you create a new document, you use a template to set formatting and program options for the document. The default template in Microsoft Word is called normal.dot. Users are expected to add their text, as well as title and header info, logos, and formatting improvements.

The normal.dot template saves time by presetting such things as page orientation, margins, and column layout to speed up your work processes. In Microsoft Office, you can save any document as a new template. Upon completion of your first balance sheet, project plan, maintenance contract, and so on, you will almost certainly have to create another very similar document. Why not save it as a template and give yourself a head start next time?

Using custom templates, you will be able to produce future documents much more quickly than by creating them from scratch. Also, seeing this past work allows you to focus more on the process and make incremental improvements without reinventing the wheel or wasting a lot of time with formatting. This approach evolves the quality of your work because you have captured not just the information within a document, but the also steps involved in its creation.

# Corroborate

The Internet is often compared to the great libraries of the world, but some things make this new learning platform vastly different from the libraries of old. Today's Internet is unequaled in terms of the amount of information that can be found relatively easily; however, this new medium brings its own set of unique issues to the scene.

Because almost anyone with access to a phone line, modem, and computer can publish on the Internet, there is a much greater need for corroboration. The potential for disseminating questionable information is high, and a reader must regard any information or data on the Internet as potentially false. Nonetheless, it is still a wonderful place to find raw material for research; the content just needs to be corroborated with caution.

### Four Techniques for Testing Information Integrity

Decide on the kind of information you want—opinions, reasoned arguments, statistics, narratives, eyewitness reports, or descriptions—and then put the information you find to the following tests:

❑ **Authorship** (for both persons and organizations): Is the author clearly identified? If a person, is his or her occupation, title, and funding source indicated?

Looking at the URL may help the reader know whether the content is from an educational institution, an individual, a government organization, or a business.

❑ **Credibility:** Consider the reputation and credentials of the author and publisher of the site.

❑ **Timeliness:** Find out when the information you find on a Website was created before you decide whether it is of value to you. Stock market predictions made in 1999 have very little value when viewed in the context of the 2003 market!

❑ **Objectivity:** Beware of slanted, biased, politically distorted work. Axe grinding makes a lot of heat and sparks, but not much light.

If you find content that is too good to be true, it probably isn't true. Look for other sources that corroborate, and never use information that you cannot verify.

### Triangulate Your Sources

Find at least three sources that agree, and if the sources do not agree, do further research to find out the range of opinion or disagreement before you draw your conclusions. Reporters call this method triangulating your sources, and they use it because it protects their credibility and often leads to new levels of awareness.

# Organize

People can find patterns in data to perceive information, and information can be used to enhance knowledge. We always want more data and information, but today we verge on information overload, so we need better ways to find patterns. Devising a careful plan to organize your information resources will allow you to keep high levels of information and data input without being crippled by information overload.

Consider how difficult it is to find a document that you created on your own computer 6 to 12 months ago. To find this document, you may need to remember its name and where you stored it on your local or network drive. The addition of metadata to a document vastly increases your ability to retrieve it for future use when you need it. Applying relevant metadata to content is often called indexing.

Common types of metadata include the format of the document (e.g., Word, PowerPoint, HTML, mpeg), the expected audience or users of the document, the author of the document, and keywords. A document's keywords can be manually defined or extracted using a piece of software. Indexing software is designed to scan a text document to retrieve and classify words that will be related to the document. Those words are then used to retrieve the document.

Indexing documents with future use in mind can be difficult, especially when individuals are accustomed to keeping information to themselves. Part of your capture process includes giving each document a name. The name is an important piece of metadata about a document. A commonly used metadata strategy is to create a data-naming convention that contains function, class, and document type.

**For example:**

**Function-Class-Document Type**

Sales-Market Analysis-Risk Matrix.doc

Technical Support-Customer Feedback-Email.eml

**Key Terms**

**Metadata:** Data that describes other data. Data dictionaries and repositories are examples of metadata. In practice, the term is used to refer to almost any descriptive entity, for example, a name and title field in a media file.

**Indexing:** Professional data capture organizations refer to the process of assigning metadata properties to an item or document as indexing.

## Secure

Security means never having to say, "I'm sorry, I seem to have lost it." Whatever security measures you decide to implement, make sure your plans include the following:

- ❑ Antivirus protection
- ❑ Regular backups
- ❑ Offsite storage of backups

As an advocate for sharing knowledge, my key role for security plans is to make sure I am always able to easily find and retask any content I've ever created. For my offsite document backup, I often use free Web-based e-mail accounts like HotMail to store my best documents. Simply blind carbon copying my latest document to my Web-based e-mail account when I send it to my boss gives me a fairly safe backup—one that I control.

## Analyze

> *No amount of sophistication is going to allay the fact that all your knowledge is about the past and all your decisions are about the future.*
>
> —Ian E. Wilson

As knowledge workers, information comes to us as diversely scattered elements. We compile this data into meaningful patterns of information through analysis. We then filter the information through our own unique set of beliefs and assumptions. Ideally, the analysis of this filtered information provides a valid basis for action—it becomes knowledge.

Every company has tacit knowledge embedded into its culture, and the company's knowledge workers provide the nodes or entry points through which information is received and then processed into knowledge. Some common analysis tools include system archetypes, comparison matrices, experimental studies, and computer modeling software. All of these tools can be used to improve your ability to find the business critical knowledge that is buried in your information and data.

## Collaborate

**Collaboration:** A human social skill that enables us to work as teams to achieve more than we could accomplish alone.

Collaboration is usually the product of one or more common goals, values, needs, ideals, visions, or interests. Collaboration groups consist of formal or informal, often self-organized, groups of employees who possess complementary knowledge and share interest in particular problems, processes, or projects in their organization. Collaborative communication is a critical part of a good personal KM strategy. It may take place between two people one-on-one and at meetings or among people via phone, e-mail, newsletters, or a company whiteboard. Wherever ideas are exchanged, they grow.

According to a 2001 InformationWeek survey on information sharing and collaboration, more than nine out of ten business and IT executives indicated that collaboration—the sharing of business information within a company—"will increase sales opportunities," and about half say it will cut costs. In fact, the survey participants agreed that "companies need to partner with suppliers and customers to develop the right products, find the right markets, and deliver goods on time without stockpiling huge inventories." Collecting valuable information and data can be difficult, costly, and time consuming, and the perishable nature of information makes sharing vitally important.

> **The Gartner Group claims that "By 2005, your enterprise will be collaborative . . . or it won't exist at all."**

Viking warriors believed that when one of their men died honorably, he was sent to Valhalla. In Valhalla, food and drink would be plentiful. A boar would be consumed every day and re-created every night, providing unlimited food. Sounds like infinite resources.

In a knowledge-based economy, an organization's ability to create new knowledge represents its most valuable resource, and attention is the currency you use to build up that resource.

The Vikings knew that when they shared their food and drink with someone in life, their loss was the other's gain. That is probably the origin of their hope for infinite resources in the afterlife. Sharing your knowledge, on the other hand, is not a zero-sum game. Unlike conventional assets, knowledge grows when it is shared. The main limitation to infinite knowledge growth is the currency of the information economy—attention.

**Metcalfe's Law**
Utility = (Nodes)$^2$

Robert Metcalfe founded 3Com Corporation and designed the ethernet protocol for computer networks. With the boom of the Internet, Robert Metcalfe gained new fame for creating Metcalfe's Law, which states that ***the usefulness of a network equals the square of the number of users.***

Remember that the goal of your KM strategy is to increase your productivity, innovation, and creative output in order to outdistance your competitors. Your personal network of resources is a key tool for achieving that goal. You can make Metcalfe's Law work for you by sharing your information, both formally and informally, with the brightest minds around you. Just be careful not to overinvest your attention. Like any valid currency, attention is finite, and that is what makes it so valuable.

### Additional Learning Resources

- ❑ *The Design of INQUIRING SYSTEMS: Basic Concepts of Systems and Organization*, by C.W. Churchman (1971)

- ❑ *The Attention Economy: Understanding the New Currency of Business*, by Thomas H. Davenport, John C. Beck (2001)

- ❑ *Envisioning Information*, by Edward R. Tufte (1990)

- ❑ *Visual Explanations: Images and Quantities, Evidence and Narrative*, by Edward R. Tufte (1997)

- ❑ *The Visual Display of Quantitative Information*, by Edward R. Tufte (2001)

- ❑ *The Internet After the Fad*, http://americanhistory.si.edu/csr/comphist/montic/metcalfe. htm, by Robert Metcalfe (1996)

 **Test Your Knowledge**

## Discussion Questions

1. What are the six action elements of your info workflow?

2. What should you remember when creating documents?

3. What are the four techniques for testing information integrity?

4.  What do cutting-edge companies pursue today?

5.  What is involved in building a KM culture?

6.  Is measurement/metrics important to KM? Why?

7.  What was required to end London's cholera epidemic of 1854?

## Review Questions

1. All business _____ involve creation, dissemination, renewal, and application of knowledge toward meeting the goals of the business.

2. It is critical to avoid focusing on _____ while disregarding how people in organizations actually go about acquiring, sharing, and creating new knowledge.

3. _____ transform information and data into knowledge by applying context and judgment.

4. KM seeks to develop a _____ that helps spread the vital knowledge of individuals or groups across organizations in ways that directly affect the bottom line.

5. Many companies are now asking their _____ to explore knowledge management because they've heard that KM is the next big competitive advantage.

6. Other organizations have realized the importance of _____ but are still years away from implementing a solution that filters down to the tactical level.

7. Personal KM should be approached with a _____ _____, documenting what you hope to achieve and what your expectations are.

8. An open and vibrant _____ network and dialogue forum is your best bet for driving forward innovation.

9. _____ that are not accurately, eloquently, and effectively delivered are rarely implemented.

10. The _____ process provides your system with the actual information and data that you have deemed worthy of inclusion in your system.

11. The _____ template saves time, by presetting such things as page orientation, margins, and column layout to speed up your work processes.

12. The _____ is often compared to the great libraries of the world.

13. People can find patterns in data to _____ information, and information can be used to enhance knowledge.

14. Common types of_____ include the format of the document (e.g., Word, PowerPoint, HTML, mpeg), the expected audience or users of the document, the author of the document, and keywords.

15. _____ _____ consist of formal or informal, often self-organized, groups of employees who possess complementary knowledge and share interest in particular problems, processes, or projects in their organization.

16. Remember that the goal of your _____ strategy is to increase your productivity, innovation, and creative output in order to outdistance your competitors.

## Chapter Vocabulary

**Best practices:** Techniques believed to constitute a paradigm of excellence in a particular field.

**Catalyst:** An element that initiates or accelerates a change.

**Causality:** The action or power of a cause, in producing its effect.

**Collaboration:** A human social skill that enables us to work as teams to achieve more than we could accomplish alone.

**Context:** That which surrounds and gives meaning to a situation or event.

**Corroborate:** To strengthen, support, or confirm with other evidence.

**Dialogue forum:** Medium for the open exchange/clash of ideas.

**Disinformation:** Deliberately misleading information.

**Eloquent:** Expressing yourself readily, clearly, and effectively with fluency and power.

**Indexing:** Professional data capture organizations refer to the process of assigning metadata properties to an item or document as indexing.

**Innovation:** A new device, process, or idea created through study, experimentation, and insight.

**Metadata:** Data that describes other data. Data dictionaries and repositories are examples of metadata. In practice, the term is used to refer to almost any descriptive entity (e.g., a name and title field in a media file).

**Metcalfe's Law:** States that the usefulness of a network equals the square of the number of users; utility $= (\text{nodes})^2$.

**Metrics:** The application of statistics and mathematical analysis to a specified endeavor.

**Quantitative:** Relating to number or quantity.

**System:** A group of interacting, interrelated, or interdependent components working together as a unit.

**Workflow:** Step-by-step process and progress of work.

# Capture and Corroborate

*For myself, I found that I was fitted for nothing so well as for the study of Truth; as having a mind nimble and versatile enough to catch the resemblances of things—and at the same time steady enough to fix and distinguish their subtler differences; as being gifted by nature with desire to seek, patience to doubt, fondness to meditate, slowness to assert, readiness to consider, carefulness to dispose and set in order; and as being a man that neither affects what is new nor admires what is old, and that hates every kind of imposture.*

—Francis Bacon, 1605

### Chapter Three Learning Objectives
- ❑ Learn a simple method for avoiding e-mail overload.
- ❑ Recognize how storing and managing information facilitates incremental improvement.
- ❑ Practice a policy of corroborating information before using it.
- ❑ Build a communication triage strategy to prevent information overload.

## Capture

When planning how to capture knowledge, don't forget that it is also prudent to capture any information that could later become knowledge. It is more economical to capture knowledge along with other information than trying to separate the two.

There are many ways to capture information and knowledge as it passes across your desk or computer screen. It is important that you value this information enough to capture it. Statistical data that are sent to you along with everyone else in your group may appear to have little value, but it could be useful if you applied your knowledge and understanding to it.

When you consider your future understanding, experiences, and knowledge, can you truly say that something that seems useless today will never be of value to you? Absolutely not! I'm sure that some people over the years have thought that my personal knowledgebase should have had "Sanford and Son" stamped on it because of all the junk it contained, but you never know when a worthless-looking bit of information or template will end up in your presentation to the senior management of your company. In today's business environment, disk space is cheap and quick delivery is often what separates the winners from the losers.

E-mail is a growing source of information and knowledge exchange in most jobs, but it is also an area of concern for corporate lawyers; therefore, most companies have a limit as to how long an e-mail will be retained on the corporate e-mail server. Also, some corporations are actually looking at e-mail systems where the e-mail expires regardless of where it is stored. This narrow view attempts to insulate the corporation against any possibility of being sued but reduces the ability to communicate to partners, vendors, and customers. It is an extremely risky strategy to say the least.

## Cost of Capture

When looking at the cost of capturing information, it is truly cheaper to capture everything coming in than to try and make a judgment call as to its value. This excludes junk mail; I'm referring to reports and information specific to business.

**Dialogue**

What are some ways that you can capture information that comes to you in an office environment?

How do I manage all of the paper?

Let's start with the basics: If e-mail is the main source of information flowing into your job, then how do you store it? The simplest way is to develop a series of subdirectories that correspond to the information flow. For instance, use the project names for the projects in which you are involved or interested. Start with an umbrella directory that contains all of the other directories. This makes backups easier.

As e-mails come in, they can be sorted by project or interest group and stored in your directory structure. This method may seem a little crude, but it enables you to manage large amounts of information with relatively simple capture techniques. Directory-structured information management also makes for easier retrieval.

To estimate our return on investment (ROI) for capturing data, we must look toward information usage. Your ability to compete in today's marketplace is determined by your ability to solve your organizational problems. The problem may be tactical or strategic, but either way your performance is based on how you solve the issue and how you document what you did. Do not be deceived, documentation counts. In tactical positions, people convince themselves that documentation is a tedious waste of time. Do not fall into this trap! Use documentation work as an opportunity to demonstrate your ability to make the solution to an issue reproducible. This approach can be a very fast road to increasing your prestige and compensation.

### Incremental Improvements

It has often been said that we are our own toughest critics. An individual's first attempt at describing or analyzing a subject is rarely the work for which they are recognized. It requires feedback, rewrites, and corroboration before the work reaches a noticeable quality level. Rarely does an employee have the time to continue refining an idea, document, or analysis until it is up to that noticeable quality level. What is possible is to continue using an idea, document, or analysis in different settings, continually improving it until it is truly noticeable. Therefore, it is important to not overfilter the information that you and your peers create; save it in your knowledgebase instead.

# Dealing with Information Overload

Some say that too much information is having a negative effect on the health, well-being, and cognitive ability of people today. This problem is often referred to as *information overload.* That term may be something of a misnomer because it leads one to believe that too much information is the problem, when actually the problem is one of attention.

The same thing often happens when we hear people talk about the information economy. In today's knowledge-rich business world, the most valuable resource is not information—it is attention. There is a nearly infinite amount of information available today, and as the amount of information grows, the value (and scarcity) of attention just keeps increasing. In order to maximize the value of this most valuable resource, it is critical that you develop an information triage strategy.

**Triage:** A French word, originally used by French wool traders, meaning "to sort or select." Its first recorded medical use was by Napoleon's surgeon, Baron Larrey. Combat medical triage rests on the premise that the greatest good must be accomplished for the greatest number under the varying conditions of warfare.

**Information triage:** A means to easily and quickly identify, prioritize, and categorize incoming information in every situation to develop competitive advantage.

The goal of information triage is to identify and quickly prioritize incoming information to maximize its value and minimize the loss of attention. The level of available resources, time, and economic factors are typical considerations in making triage decisions.

# Information Triage

No one disputes that the production of information is increasing dramatically. Some experts have estimated that the amount of printed information doubles every 72 days. Today, one weekday issue of the *New York Times* contains more information than the average 17th-century individual would have seen in a lifetime. In the last 30 years, more information has been produced than in the previous 5,000 years.

Knowledge workers receive large volumes of time-sensitive textual information that requires triage—rapid, approximate prioritization for subsequent action. To keep from being overloaded with unimportant information, knowledge workers must conduct information triage. Like battlefield medics sorting out casualties according to severity of injuries, a knowledge worker sorts through a huge amount of information to select information to use and think about.

The goals of information triage are to make the right decisions based on priority and then convert those decisions into action. That means prioritizing, delegating, and just ignoring some information.

*Webster's Dictionary* defines triage as "the sorting of and allocation of treatment to patients and especially battle and disaster victims according to a system of priorities designed to maximize the number of survivors." Typically, this involves sorting casualties into three categories:

- ❏ Casualties likely to survive if they receive prompt or extensive attention
- ❏ Casualties likely to survive with routine, nonurgent care
- ❏ Casualties unlikely to survive even with the maximum possible effort

For our information triage strategy, we focus on sorting incoming information into three similar categories:

- ❏ Information that needs immediate action (to do)
- ❏ Information you expect to act on later (to know)
- ❏ Information you think you may need later (to archive)

At the beginning of each day, I look at the information that has come in to me, and I handle it based on which of the three categories it best fits into. Information that doesn't fit into any of these three categories is deleted immediately. I also use some tools to make this process easier.

- ❏ **Message folders and rules:** Most e-mail systems will allow you to create folders within the e-mail system and automatically route incoming messages to those folders based on criteria such as priority code, text in the subject line, or sender's e-mail address. Often, these rules can be used to categorize and move your "to know" and "to archive" information into subfolders. This frees up your attention to focus on the higher-priority "to do" items.

- ❏ **Color coding:** Some e-mail systems allow you to further organize your inbox using color. You can set messages sent directly to you alone in one color and messages on which you are carbon-copied in another color. You can set a special color for messages from your boss and a separate color for messages containing read receipts. The possibilities are practically endless. Don't underestimate the value of noticing something first. Remember that attention is the currency you invest in your social network, so use it wisely.

❑ **Unsubscribing to spam and blocking senders:** When it comes to spam, it pays to be ruthless with repeat offenders. There are too many ways to get put on the mailing lists of spammers these days to think that anyone can be completely free of spam; however, you can usually follow a link within the e-mail to unsubscribe from the mailing list. Those unsavory entrepreneurs who keep sending spam to you anyway or who don't offer the option to unsubscribe can simply be blocked from sending you any mail at all. Remember, the goal is not to eliminate spam but to maximize your available attention by minimizing the time you waste dealing with spam.

## Information Capture Sources

Effective information triage empowers you to capture vast quantities of information from a wide array of sophisticated and ad hoc sources, all occurring in chaotic circumstances. Once your information triage strategy is in place, the amount of information and data that you can handle will increase by an order of magnitude. This allows you the time and attention to gather information from many more sources. The sources you choose should be evaluated carefully to ensure that they meet your needs. Here are some examples of common information resources you may want to integrate into your strategy:

❑ **Trade magazines:** Contain product reviews, press releases, demonstrations, and lab tests, all of which help you make a decision to move into new processes and technologies. Beware of biased and flawed product evaluations, driven by rapid publication cycles and advertising money. Triangulate your sources!

❑ **Newsgroups:** Newsgroups have been popular since before the Web was created. By the end of 1997, there were more than 50,000 newsgroups. Some are moderated and some are not, and no single online service hosts them. They originate from many sources and are hosted on many systems that are known collectively as the **Usenet network**.

Newsgroup postings represent the wisdom, experiences, and opinions of millions of people around the world on just about any topic imaginable. No one group controls or filters what appears in a newsgroup. Although everything should be taken with a grain of salt, newsgroups can nevertheless be extremely valuable. They often provide the best source of highly specific and unbiased information for problem solving. They also have the advantage of interactivity. Posting a question on a newsgroup can often deliver that hard-to-find technical answer within minutes and often leads to valuable new business contacts.

❑ **Discussion forums:** Discussion forums are very much like Usenet newsgroups, but they are typically Web based and often provide a searchable online archive of past messages. Because of the low implementation cost, these forums can be found on almost any type of Website. Unfortunately, the low barriers to entry also result in a greater need for filtering and corroboration.

❑ **Web portals:** A web portal provides access to a variety of services, such as Web searching, news, white and yellow pages directories, free e-mail, discussion groups, online shopping and links to other sites. Although the term was initially used to refer to general-purpose sites, it is increasingly being used to refer to vertical market sites that offer the same services, but only to a particular industry such as banking, insurance, or computers.

❑ **Mailing lists** (a.k.a. e-zines): Automated e-mail systems on the Internet, which are organized by subject matter. There are more than 10,000 such lists covering almost any subject imaginable. New users generally subscribe by sending an e-mail with the word "subscribe" in it and subsequently receive all new postings made to the list automatically.

> **TIP:** Mailing list e-mails are an excellent example of the type of information you will want to have automatically routed to a custom inbox subfolder using message rules.

❑ **Web search engines and directories:** Sites that maintain databases about the contents of other Websites. Most sites are free and are paid for by advertising. Yahoo! was the first search site to gain worldwide attention. It differs from most other search sites because actual people create a hierarchical directory by subject to index the content. As a result, Yahoo! and similar sites are technically called *directories* rather than search engines. Most search engine sites use software called *crawlers* to automatically find and index Website content; however, there is a growing trend toward pay-for-listing search engines.

## Tips for Using Search Engines and Directories

When preparing to use a Web search engine or directory, first define your search and pick your tool. Before you begin your search, you should always consider your search strategy and have a clear idea about your goals.

For instance, if you want to:

❑ **Browse a specific subject area:** Try using a directory like Yahoo! or Magellan.

❑ **Search Usenet:** Use DejaNews, AltaVista, or HotBot.

❑ **Search document properties like titles, URLs, keywords:** Use WebCrawler, Yahoo!, or AltaVista.

❑ **Locate an obscure document:** Use Google, AltaVista, or Northern Lights.

A few quick "gotchas" to watch out for:

❑ Don't automatically start with your favorite search engine.

❑ Don't assume that all search engines produce similar results.

❑ Don't assume that relevance rankings from the different search tools will match up.

# Corroborate

*Caveat lector: Let the reader beware.*

Sometimes it can be difficult to be certain of the reliability of the information you collect. It is important for you to remain objective when assessing the nature of the information, no matter what opinion you may hold about the general situation. You should aim to obtain the best information possible under the circumstances. This does not mean that you must always reach the highest standard before submitting information, but it does mean that you should do your best to corroborate all of the information available to you.

Unfortunately, there is no easy checklist to consult to see if a Web page is credible. One of the most popular forms of bad information on the Internet, especially e-mail, is the passing along of urban legends.

**Urban legends:** Often cautionary or moralistic, yet untrue, stories that are passed along by sincere people who believe them and feel the need to help others become informed.

Urban legends may arise from malice or simple misunderstanding. They become a problematic source of misinformation when sincere, but mistaken, people repeat them. Everybody makes mistakes, so check the validity of everything you read before you put your belief in it and use it.

Urban legends, chain letters, and most hoax messages all have a very similar pattern. They usually have three recognizable parts:

1. The bait
2. The threat
3. The request

1. *The bait.* To catch readers' interest and get them to stick with the con, urban legends try to engage readers' greed, suspicion, sympathy, or fear. Watch for subject lines such as "Make Money Fast," "Virus Alert," or "A Little Girl Is Dying."

2. *The threat.* After you've taken the bait, you get to the threat. Some threats are used to warn you about the terrible things that will happen if you don't keep forwarding the message. Others play on greed or sympathy to get you to pass the message on. The threat often contains official or technical-sounding language to get you to believe it is real.

3. *The request.* E-mailed urban legends try to convince you to "Distribute this letter to as many people as possible." They never mention clogging the Internet, divulging private contact info to a long list of strangers, or the fact that the message is a fake; they only want you to pass it on to others. Before unwittingly helping someone "spread the word," it is a good idea to make sure the real goal isn't to "spread the manure."

## Why Send Out This Junk in the First Place?

Among other reasons, people send hoax messages to:

- ❑ See how far a letter will go.
- ❑ Harass someone (include an e-mail address and ask everyone to send mail).
- ❑ Bilk people out of money using a pyramid scheme or other types of fraud.
- ❑ Gather an e-mail list of "likely" targets for future scams.
- ❑ Kill some other chain letter (e.g., "Make Money Fast").
- ❑ Damage a person's or organization's reputation.
- ❑ Infect other PCs with keyboard loggers or other nefarious code.

If you suspect a story to be an urban legend or hoax message, you can try one of the following resources. Chances are that you are not the first to receive it.

- ❑ Internet ScamBusters: www.scambusters.org
- ❑ The Urban Legend Combat Kit: www.netsquirrel.com/combatkit
- ❑ The Museum of Hoaxes: www.museumofhoaxes.com
- ❑ The Urban Legend Archive: www.urbanlegends.com
- ❑ Urban Legends Reference Pages: www.snopes2.com

Also, the larger antivirus companies have Web pages containing information about known viruses and hoaxes.

In addition to the four techniques for testing information integrity introduced earlier (i.e., authorship, credibility, timeliness, and objectivity), you may also want to consider the following factors when corroborating your information:

- ❑ The reputation of the publishing authority
- ❑ The level of detail
- ❑ The presence of contradictions

Evaluating information usually consists of weighing several criteria together, so you will need to assess how important each aspect is on a case-by-case basis. Remember that it is often not possible to obtain information of the highest quality, but this does not mean that you cannot use it. Instead, the quality of your information will be a factor when the time comes to select how you wish to use it.

Developing criteria for filtering information found on the Internet can be an excellent beginning for becoming a well-informed consumer of information. Question everything you read. Triangulate using other sources that can authenticate or corroborate your research. Learn to be skeptical and watch out for urban legends.

**Dialogue**

How many of the following rumors have you heard?

Can you pick out the ones that are true? (50%)

❑ Children who go swimming less than one hour after eating will get cramps and drown.

❑ In 1919, a killing wave of molasses swept through Boston.

❑ Chewing gum takes seven years to pass through the human digestive system.

❑ A couple of kids sign up an imaginary boy for a free yearly ice cream cone. Years later, they receive a draft notice for their invisible friend.

❑ The state of Missouri named a stretch of highway adopted by the Ku Klux Klan the Rosa Parks Highway.

❑ Drugged college students awaken in ice-filled bathtubs to discover organ thieves have stolen one of their kidneys.

❑ Rice thrown at weddings is dangerous to birds.

## Additional Learning Resources

❑ *Validation and Verification of Knowledge Based Systems: Theory, Tools and Practice*, by Anca Vermesan & Frans Coenen

❑ *Attacking Faulty Reasoning: A Practical Guide to Fallacy-Free Arguments*, by T. Edward Damer

❑ http://skeptic.com—A collection of strange beliefs, amusing deceptions, and dangerous delusions

❑ www.calpress.com/pdf_files/what&why.pdf—A detailed overview by Peter Facione of the nature of critical thinking.

## Test Your Knowledge

## Discussion Questions

1. What should you consider when you set out to capture knowledge and information?

2. What are some ways to capture information?

3. Is capturing the information and knowledge expensive? Why?

4. How often are documents created that do not require editing?

5. How does information triage work?

6. How fast is information growing in our world?

7. How do you currently maintain the information and knowledge that you use and create?

8. Have you ever used a newsgroup to find information? Was it helpful?

9. Have you ever been deceived by an urban legend?

10. Can urban legends be confirmed? How?

## Review Questions

1. It is more _____ to capture knowledge along with other information than trying to separate the two.

2. Statistical data that are sent to you along with everyone else in your group may appear to have little value, but it could be useful if you applied your _____ _____ and _____ to it.

3. E-mail is a growing source of information and knowledge in most jobs, but it is also an area of concern for _____ _____.

4. When looking at the cost of capturing information, it is truly _____ to capture everything coming in than to try and make a judgment call as to its value.

5. As _____ come in, they can be sorted by project or interest group and stored in your directory structure.

6. To estimate our _____ _____ _____ (ROI) for capturing data, we must look toward information usage.

7. In _____ positions, people convince themselves that action counts, not documentation.

8. Rarely does an employee have the time to continue refining an idea, document, or analysis until it is to that _____ _____ level.

9. Some say that _____ _____ _____ is having a negative effect on the health, well-being, and cognitive ability of people today.

10. The same thing often happens when we hear people talk about the _____ _____.

11. The goal of _____ _____ is to identify and quickly prioritize incoming information to maximize its value and minimize the loss of attention.

12. Some experts have estimated that the amount of printed information doubles every _____ days.

13. To keep from being overloaded with _____ information, knowledge workers must conduct information triage.

14. Once your information triage _____ is in place, the amount of information and data that you can handle will increase by an order of magnitude.

15. Posting a question on a _____ can often deliver that hard-to-find technical answer within minutes.

16. Sometimes it can be difficult to be certain of the _____ of the information you collect.

17. One of the most popular forms of bad information on the Internet, especially e-mail, is the passing along of _____ _____.

## Chapter Vocabulary

**Ad hoc sources:** Sources formed for or concerned with one specific purpose, often biased.

**Contradictions:** Opposition among multiple conflicting forces or ideas.

**Incremental:** One of a series of regular additions or contributions.

**Information overload:** A state where the individual is no longer able to effectively process the amount of information to which he or she is exposed.

**Information triage:** A means to easily and quickly identify, prioritize, and categorize incoming information in every situation to develop competitive advantage.

**Return on investment (ROI):** For a given use of money, the ROI is how much return, usually profit or cost saving, results.

**Spam:** Unsolicited commercial messages sent in bulk from strangers to strangers in hopes of random sales.

**Strategic:** Highly important to or an integral part of a long-term plan.

**Tactical:** Relating to operations that are smaller and of less long-term significance than strategic operations.

**Triage:** A system used to allocate a scarce commodity, such as food, to only those who are capable of deriving the greatest benefit from it.

**Urban legend:** A tale of contemporary folklore that purports to be true and is often designed to elicit an emotional response from the audience.

**Usenet network:** Worldwide bulletin board system, probably the largest decentralized information utility in existence.

**Web directories:** Websites providing links to information organized into categorical, alphabetical hierarchies.

**Web portals:** Websites that serve as specialized starting points to other destinations or activities on the Web.

**Web search engines:** Websites (actually programs) that act as card catalogs for the Internet; search engines attempt to index and locate desired information by searching for the keywords a user specifies.

# Organize and Secure

*I never commit to memory anything that can easily be looked up
in a book.*

—Albert Einstein

**Chapter Four Learning Objectives**

❑ Create documents that are RARE: readable, available, retrievable, and electronic.

❑ Know how to define your metadata to support accurate retrieval of your documents.

❑ Learn about a good tool for improving document retrieval on your PC.

❑ Learn to take personal responsibility to protect your most vital information.

## Organize

How do you find information that you created two years ago? How do you search your own personal work for information that might be relevant on your current project? Where do you turn to find the critical e-mail that contains promised but undelivered services? What do you use to quickly catalog the 1,000 documents that your law firm has just received electronically during discovery of a nationwide product liability case? Even if you find that long-lost document, will it be in a format that you can view with your current applications? Today's high-end document management systems often store documents on huge optical disks aiming for a 30-year lifespan. Want to bet we'll all be using vastly different word processing applications by then?

Organizing information to solve problems is at the heart of all management information system (MIS)/IT jobs, and knowing ways to leverage tools can help secure your career in any field. When planning your strategy for organizing your archived information, make certain that you create documents that are RARE: readable, available, retrievable, and electronic.

**Readable:** Documents stored in obsolete and unreadable formats are worse than useless—they are a liability. Ensure that your archived information and data are in formats that will preserve their possibility for reuse, and verify annually that any items you intend to store for the long term remain readable. I archive my information into a combination of text files, HTML, and Word documents.

**Available:** You can't reuse it if it isn't there. All archiving plans should include components to ensure that files are regularly backed up offsite and scanned for viruses.

**Retrievable:** You can't reuse it if you can't find it. Apply a well-thought-out and consistent taxonomy to your data and information. This part is often easier said than done.

**Electronic:** Too many people consider electronic documents as merely a way to create good-looking paper documents. In fact, a better view would be to see paper documents as merely a handy way to advertise the real product—the electronic document.

## Metadata Improves Your Accuracy

As the amount of unstructured text out there steadily grows in size, intelligent information retrieval techniques are all the more important for keeping you ahead of the pack. Metadata is the key component to allowing effective information retrieval. By describing the essential aspects of text, such as author, language, subject, publication, popularity rating, and revision dates, metadata improves the precision of your searching. It is also helpful for classifying and routing content, grouping for aggregate analysis, and determining the need for additional processing, such as translation.

Remember that keyword searching is a powerful, yet crude tool for locating valuable information sources. Initially, what you receive as a result is rarely the answer you were looking for; usually it is a list of documents that provide further clues to refining your search more.

## Manual vs. Automated Indexing

Sometimes the job of analyzing content and creating metadata categories can be automated, and in other cases human intelligence is required. Manual systems typically reflect a human understanding of the information and of the way people normally associate topics. The Internet portal pioneer Yahoo!, for example, employs a cadre of categorizers to improve the accuracy of the company's search engine, but the Yahoo! approach is time consuming and costly, and they can never hope to index a significant portion of the Web. In addition, human categorizers are often inconsistent in assigning categories.

Purely automated approaches to metadata indexing can be the fastest and easiest way to index your metadata. Although the cost savings can be significant, automated indexing systems often fail to deliver the combination of accuracy and precision that today's knowledge workers need to be effective.

There are pros and cons to both types of indexing, and often the best solution is a combination of the two. Try your best to strike a balance between cost and accuracy. However you choose to index your metadata, you will still need to store it.

In storing metadata, there are typically two schools of thought: (1) store the metadata directly within the document or (2) manage it separately from the documents in a relational database. HTML documents typically store metadata internally in *metatags*, or XML and Word documents store the metadata in document properties. Data warehouses and commercial document management systems use highly scalable relational databases to store metadata.

### Weapon of Choice

In order to maintain document/metadata integrity and facilitate easy offsite backups, I prefer archiving my data in Microsoft Word documents. In order to make sure that I add metadata to every document I create, I have customized my installation of Microsoft Word to prompt me for document properties whenever I save a new Word document. I even convert Web pages to Word documents because I like the way it keeps the text, images, and metadata all in one single document format. Another advantage of using Microsoft Word's flexible document format is that you can utilize some of the powerful features of Word to add value to your knowledgebase. Some of these features include:

❑ **Version control:** Provides a database that keeps track of the revisions made to a document. Word supports two ways of working with different versions of documents: saving versions of a document in a single file and comparing differences between different documents.

❑ **AutoSummarize:** This advanced Word feature is designed to "automatically summarize the key points in a document." This is useful for two reasons: (1) it can create a summary of a document a user is producing (e.g., for an abstract or executive summary), and (2) it can be used to summarize electronic documents that a user receives from other sources.

❑ **Online collaboration:** Connects the desktop to the Web, allowing people to publish documents, analyze data, exchange comments, and collaborate online.

## Microsoft Index Services

Microsoft added an integrated search engine to the operating system in their Windows 2000 platform. Index Server brings full-text indexing and searching to your fingertips. Almost no administration is required to get Index Server started indexing your documents. Whenever a file stored on the system is changed, added, or deleted, Index Server automatically rebuilds the index. This ensures that you always have access to the most up-to-date information.

> **Believe it or not, Index Server can even index files stored on any file system accessible to a Windows NT Server. This includes Novell NetWare and Unix systems.**

Index Server can index not only your HTML and text files, but also Microsoft Word, Excel, and PowerPoint files. Any other document type can be indexed using the open IFilter interface. An optical character recognition (OCR) IFilter will even crawl through your directories of scanned images (Group IV tagged image file format [TIFF]), run OCR on them, and create index records based on the results.

Index Server also provides access to document properties such as author, in both HTML and Microsoft Office documents. Index Server includes support for seven languages: English, French, German, Dutch, Spanish, Italian, and Swedish. All languages include full linguistic stemming, to allow for fuzzy searches on all tenses of a verb. This means that searches on keywords like *plan* will retrieve documents containing words like *planning*.

Microsoft's Index Server is not only available for Windows 2000 but is also an add-on service to the Internet Information Server (IIS) that enables indexing of document properties and contents on the IIS Web server. After the IIS server indexes documents within directories included in its catalogs, users can query the Index Server with their Web browsers to search for selected document contents or properties. Responses to user queries are presented back to the client's Web browser as a series of HTML links to the documents containing the query properties or contents.

The Microsoft Index Server facilitates information location by indexing both contents and properties of all specified documents managed by the IIS server—not only index text and HTML files, but common document format files as well (such as .doc and .xls). With add-on filters, Index Server will even OCR and index Group IV TIFFs. The virtual directories assigned in the Internet Information Server are used by the Index Server to control indexing.

Index Server automatically creates the index on the selected document directories and is notified when documents are added or deleted from the selected directories. Changes made to documents, or the addition of new documents since the last indexing session, are automatically added to the catalog. The indexing process is designed to operate as a background task to minimize system resource use while running and requires no input from the administrator to complete the indexing operation.

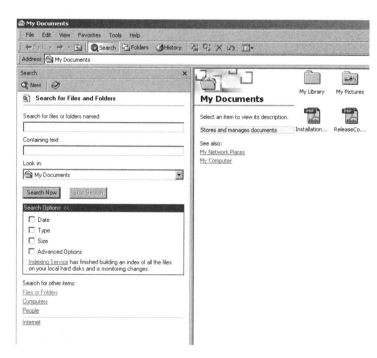

FIGURE 4.1 **Starting Index Services on your Win2000 PC.**

After launching Windows Explorer, choose Search from the toolbar. Under "Search Options" you will find "Index Services."

Index Server is completely integrated with the IIS and Windows NT Server security, providing substantial control over access to indexed documents. Website clients searching through the indexed documents are only allowed to view documents that they have permission to access.

By enabling Index Services, you will be able to define directories on your PC that you wish to have full content indexed. Full-content indexing allows the user to search documents using a keyword search.

By choosing search words more carefully, you can narrow your search to a few documents.

Selecting "Query the Catalog" from the catalog tree will bring up the "Indexing Service Query Form." This is an HTML document that can be customized to fit your needs.

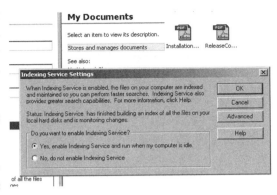

FIGURE 4.2 **Enabling Index Services.**

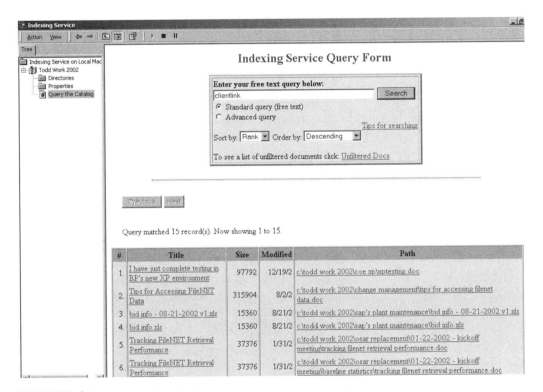

FIGURE 4.3 **Querying the Catalogs.**

## Query Restrictions

A range of query restrictions are available in Index Server, enabling users to specify one or more restrictions in any combination. The types of query restrictions include:

- ❑ Words, phrases, and complete sentences
- ❑ Document types (such as only .doc or .txt)
- ❑ Textual properties (such as words within an abstract or author property)

❑ Boolean operators against document content or property values (such as AND, OR, and NOT)

❑ Wild-card operators (* and ?)

❑ Numeric operators against constants (such as using the < operator against a document date)

❑ Proximity of words or phrases

❑ Ranked by match quality

## Advanced Queries

There are five main types of queries:

❑ Free-text queries

❑ Phrase queries

❑ Pattern-matching queries

❑ Relational queries

❑ Vector-space queries

### Case Study: Indexing Dot-Matrix Check Registry

A large energy corporation was faced with the need to manage payment of pension checks to retirees and their dependants. This need arose after a merger and the discovery that the newly merged company's pension payment history consisted of a dot-matrix printout provided from the bank. After many heated discussions with bank management, it was determined that the corporation must find a way to store and index six years' worth of printouts. The total project consisted of approximately 75,000 pages of dot-matrix-printed check registers. Each page contained the payment information for approximately 63 checks, including check date, check number, recipient's Social Security number, recipient's name, and check amount. Future growth was expected to be 12,000 to 15,000 pages annually to be added to this system, and the total number of users that required access was two to five people.

The initial assessment from the internal IT department was a three-month project with total costs in the range of $180,000 to $220,000 with a $35,000 to $50,000 annual system maintenance cost and $30,000 to $40,000 for annual future document capture. The bid only included indexing for check number and Social Security number, and it was stated that accuracy was expected to be near 95%.

Faced with a five-year cost of $505,000 to $670,000, the human resources (HR) group turned to their internal HRIS group for possible ideas. Several ideas were offered, but the option that promised the best chance for success was based on Microsoft's Index Services for IIS. The plan consisted of the following points:

❑ Scan all of the existing pages with the scanner configured to build a new TIFF for each page.

❑ Copy all of the TIFFs into a directory on a Web server running Microsoft IIS.

❑ Configure Microsoft's Index Server to OCR and index all of the TIFFs.

❑ Build a Web page that pointed to the Check Registry Catalog.

❑ Give NT security access to the HR users that needed access to the Check Registry Catalog.

❑ Train the users on the Web query functionality.

The HR leadership approved the project, but the internal IT group would not agree to execute the plan. After a short delay, it was decided that the HRIS group had the technical expertise to complete the project, so they undertook it. The project was completed on an existing Web server in eight days at a total cost of $17,730. The annual system maintenance cost was $16,500 and $1,047 for the first year's future document capture. The five-year cost of ownership is expected to be between $105,000 to $115,000. This will make the savings over the originally proposed system to be $400,000 to $555,000.

Besides the financial savings to the corporation, the Index Server solution also provided better functionality by indexing all of the fields and returning accuracy of 98% to 100% (the range is based on available search information). For searches that the HR specialist was given only one field to search, such as Social Security number or check number, accuracy was found to be 98% or better. When given at least two fields, search results were 100%.

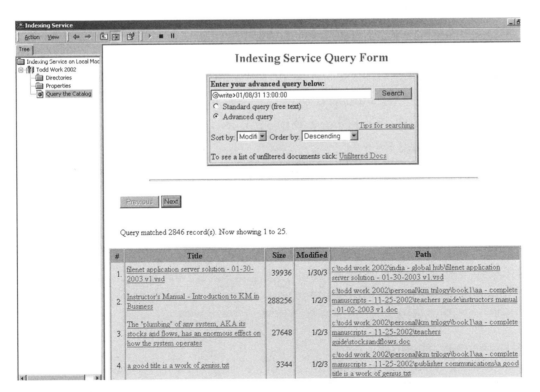

FIGURE 4.4 **Indexing Service Query Form.**

> **Worldwide, two-thirds of companies report having been hit by virus, worm, and Trojan horse assaults in the past year, and U.S. companies have a slightly higher incident rate than these global averages.**

# Secure Your Information Assets

Knowledge workers must protect their information to remain competitive. Your personal information can be used by criminals, creeps, and even co-workers to gain services, create fraudulent credit accounts, and obtain false identification. Losing access to previously created documents can slow your project delivery time by an order of magnitude. Knowledge workers typically lose their old information assets as a result of one or more of four causes:

- ❑ *User errors.* Know your interface well to avoid these errors.
- ❑ *PC changes.* Expect and plan for any equipment changes.
- ❑ *Job changes.* Make sure your personal information comes with you when you leave.
- ❑ *Malicious software.* Keep an up-to-date virus scanner on guard.

## Personal Information Security

Although recognizing the value of sharing information over hoarding it is key to KM, there is still certain information that you should never give out without a *very* good reason:

- ❑ Credit card numbers or expiration dates, unless you know the company is reputable.
- ❑ Checking account numbers or ATM personal identification numbers.
- ❑ Telephone calling card numbers.
- ❑ Social security numbers; only give this out if it is legally required.
- ❑ Driver's license numbers.
- ❑ Health information, such as your insurance, medical, and mental history, and doctor.
- ❑ Information about your home security system, such as whether you have one or your access codes; information about those who live with you and whether you live alone.
- ❑ Your age and financial information, such as your annual income, mortgage, or financial institution. In addition, you should keep track of whenever you do provide this information and to whom it was given.

## E-mail Attachment Security

E-mail attachments have gotten progressively more dangerous in recent years. You can avoid a great deal of lost time and energy by following a few simple rules.

**Rule 1:** Never, never, never open unexpected e-mail attachments that come from people you don't know. Just delete it!

**Rule 2:** If the attachment is a forwarded joke, video, audio, .vbs, .scr, or .pif file, just delete it!

**Rule 3:** If you receive an unexpected e-mail attachment from someone that you do know, check with the sender before opening it to be sure that they meant to send it and to find out what is in it. People rarely send attachments without some kind of note. Be very suspicious if the attachment isn't referred to in the message's body text.

**Rule 4:** If the attachment is a legitimate file from a known source, you should still scan it with up-to-date antivirus software before opening it.

Your antivirus program should have a mode where it will do this scan automatically—make sure that it is running. If in doubt, throw it out! If it's a legitimate file, it can always be resent, after you check with the sender.

## Stay in Contact

In today's connected world, networking accounts for most hires (85% of jobs are unadvertised, according to the Bureau of Labor Statistics), and positions rarely last until retirement. These facts make it critical for knowledge workers to personally make certain that their most valuable information resources are effectively secured. Often, the most valuable information resource is the worker's list of names and contact information for a network of peers, customers, and suppliers.

**Treat your list of contacts as an ongoing, long-term investment asset:**

- ❑ Protect it.
- ❑ Add to it frequently.
- ❑ Keep it diverse.

That means maintaining offsite backups, being dedicated to upkeep, and regularly updating virus scanning.

## Job Security

Loss of information because of an unexpected job change can leave you without contacts when you need them the most. Leaving any job is uncomfortable. Feeling like you are abandoning commitments and friendships is typical if you are leaving a job you enjoyed. For other jobs, you might be thrilled to be going and want to drop everything and run. Here's a small list of things worth making sure you hold on to:

- ❑ Analysis document templates
- ❑ Project planning document templates
- ❑ Old copies of your resume

❑ Contact lists

❑ Help files

❑ Company benefits and 401K information

Love it or hate it, your old company deserves the standard two-weeks' notice, and you will probably need that time to make sure you leave with your assets intact.

### Self-inflicted E-mail for Offline Information Access

One of the easiest ways to back up your critical information offsite is through self-inflicted e-mail. A wide variety of organizations are now offering free Web-based e-mail accounts. You can use these accounts to store document templates and keep yourself a handy document storage system that is accessible from any Web-connected browser in the world.

### Free Web-based E-mail Providers

❑ My Yahoo!—http://my.yahoo.com

❑ HotMail—www.hotmail.com

❑ Mail.com—www.mail.com

## Persistence and Discipline

Personal KM requires persistence and discipline to return value. If capture procedures are designed and implemented but not used consistently, the information that is captured will not be trusted because everyone knows that it is incomplete. Discipline is required to continually improve the capture methods that are used so that the knowledgebase will continue to grow and be retrieved from.

A decision must be made to begin, and after that you must continue sowing the information that you come in contact with into your knowledgebase. You must consistently capture the metadata following the taxonomy that you have laid out, and you must capture using your triage rules of relevance. Much like a farmer, you must sow before you can reap, but the sooner you begin, the larger the harvest.

### Additional Learning Resources

❑ http://argus-acia.com—The Argus Center for Information Architecture

❑ http://msdn.microsoft.com/library/en-us/indexsrv/html/ indexingservicestartpage_6td1.asp—Indexing Service Software Developers Kit

❑ www.searchtools.com/tools/microsoft-index.html—Directory of Index Services Resources

❑ www.infosecnews.com—The online security news service is backed by *SC Magazine.*

❑ *Safe Computing: How to Protect Your Computer, Your Body, Your Data, Your Money and Your Privacy in the Information Age*, by Tom Bentley

## Test Your Knowledge

### Discussion Questions

1. How do you find information that you created two years ago?

2. What do MIS/IT people spend most of their time doing?

3. What is the purpose of document management systems?

4. How do you organize your information?

5. What is the purpose of metadata?

6. What is the purpose of Microsoft's Index Services?

7. How do you protect your personal information?

### Review Questions

1. How do you search your own _____ _____ for information that might be relevant on your current project?

2. Today's high-end _____ _____ systems often store documents on huge optical disks aiming for a 30-year lifespan.

3. When planning your strategy for organizing archived information, you will need to focus on these key areas: _____, _____, and _____.

4. As the amount of _____ text out there steadily grows in size, intelligent information retrieval techniques are all the more important for keeping you ahead of the pack.

5. The Internet portal pioneer Yahoo!, for example, employs a cadre of categorizers to improve the accuracy of the company's _____ _____.

6. In storing _____, there are typically two schools of thought: (1) store the metadata directly within the document or (2) manage it separately from the documents in a relational database.

7. _____ _____ brings full-text indexing and searching to your fingertips.

8. Index Server can index not only your _____ and text files, but also Microsoft Word, Excel, and PowerPoint files.

9. Index Server also provides access to _____ _____, such as author, in both HTML and Microsoft Office documents.

10. After the _____ _____ indexes documents within directories included in its catalogs, users can query the Index Server with their Web browsers to search for selected document contents or properties.

11. Changes made to documents, or the addition of new documents since the last indexing session, are automatically added to the _____.

12. Index Server is completely integrated with the IIS and Windows NT Server security, providing substantial control over access to _____ _____.

13. Losing access to previously created documents can slow your _____ delivery time by an order of magnitude.

14. In today's connected world, networking accounts for most hires (_____% of jobs are unadvertised, according to the Bureau of Labor Statistics) and positions rarely last until retirement.

15. One of the easiest ways to back up your critical information offsite is the _____ _____.

16. Personal KM requires _____ and _____ to return value.

## Chapter Vocabulary

**Aggregate analysis:** Analysis of total data collected with reference to its constituent parts.

**AutoSummarize:** Word feature that automatically creates abridged versions of documents.

**Available:** State of being readily accessible.

**Boolean operators:** Logical query terms such as AND, OR, and NOT.

**Document management system:** Technology designed to facilitate the capture, storage, and sharing of electronic documents.

**Group IV tagged image file format (TIFF):** A widely used bitmapped graphics file format developed by Aldus and Microsoft that handles monochrome, gray-scale, and 8- and 24-bit color.

**Metatags:** Bits of ASCII text that describe various context aspects of a particular Web page.

**Microsoft Index Server:** Integrated search engine software included in Windows 2000.

**Optical character recognition (OCR):** The machine recognition of printed characters.

**Readable:** State of being readily intelligible.

**Retrievable:** The ability to recall at will.

**Trojan horse:** A program that appears legitimate but performs some illicit activity when it is run.

**Version control:** Used to keep track of revisions.

**Virus:** Software used to purposefully infect, damage, and/or control a computer.

**Worm:** Destructive program that replicates itself throughout disk and memory, using up the computer's memory.

# Analyze and Collaborate

*For every complex problem there is always a simple solution. And it is wrong.*

—Henry Louis Mencken (1880–1956), American editor and critic

### Chapter Five Learning Objectives

- ❑ See how abstractions are used to allow people to make appropriate use of things that are not complete.
- ❑ Understand why humans perceive things differently, based on their unique abstractions.
- ❑ Learn the five key requirements for successful collaboration.
- ❑ Build effective listening habits to promote successful collaborations.
- ❑ Learn to take personal responsibility to protect your most vital information.

For data to become information, it requires two things:

1. A logical form or arrangement
2. A context that is meaningful or at least relevant to the user

## Layers of Abstraction

Most knowledge workers spend their time involved in pattern recognition, and data are the raw material in the knowledge worker's pattern recognition process. For a pattern to emerge, there has to be some repetition of an event. Once the information set contains repeating elements (i.e., the expenses for November 26, 1998, 1999, and 2000), then we can say that a potential pattern is embedded into the information. We use layers of abstraction to make these patterns more visible.

Discovering and communicating these potential patterns in data relies on the capability to effectively create abstractions. Effective knowledge workers draw on their repertoire of abstractions to find new insights and opportunities in the available information and data patterns.

Abstraction helps us interpret and expand complex data and information patterns. Systems grow more sophisticated by growing additional layers of abstraction. For example, ancient humans conducted almost all economic dealings by barter (I'll trade my chunk of mammoth meat for your chunk of flint) or by theft. As social structures grew and increased in complexity, another layer of abstraction was added—money. This new layer created the opportunity for more and more layers of abstraction (e.g., debt, common stock, interest), which allowed the system to become increasingly complex and powerful.

Luckily for us, with layers of abstraction it is not necessary to have complete knowledge about something in order to make appropriate use of it. For instance, consider the telephone: One can enjoy talking on the phone without knowing how to design a telephone. It is not necessary to be able to build a telephone in order to use one, nor do its builders need to be able to design one. Naturally, telephone designers do not need to be able to produce the materials from which their phones are made.

Each group has different priorities for what must be known about a telephone. Each has an essential subset of detail taken from all that is available to know about the subject. Each focuses only on the essentials to a particular role, and needs only a high-level awareness of the details important to others. Organizing or digesting details using abstraction allows you to concentrate on or grasp essential patterns or to see the big picture.

The process of abstraction relies on leaving out of consideration one or more properties of a complex object so as to focus the attention on other properties. It is essentially an act of generalization, ignoring or hiding details to capture the commonalities between different instances. Surprisingly, this is a very powerful technique for problem solving and learning.

Computers use an algorithmic problem-solving approach (a set of instructions are required in order to solve a problem). Therefore, unless the specific steps that the computer needs to follow are defined, the computer cannot solve the problem. That restricts the capability of most computers to solving problems that we already understand and know how to solve.

Conversely, a human can detect and recognize complex patterns with only a minimal amount of training. This capability is incredibly useful for identifying objects and organizing our perception of complex systems and environments. We also use our pattern recognition capability to recognize situations as comparable to ones we have experienced or thought about before and then draw on our previously considered conclusions and experiences.

**Abstraction:** The process of taking away or removing characteristics from something in order to reduce it to a set of essential characteristics.

> **The process of abstraction relies on setting a goal, defining a data representation, identifying relevant features, and categorization.**

## Steps in the Abstraction Process

Defining a data representation refers to the creation of a pattern class. A pattern class describes which specific characteristics will define your abstraction.

For example, in analyzing brands of tomato paste, you are interested in a limited subset of properties such as size, color, texture, ripeness, and fragrance—these properties represent your pattern class. If you manage an Italian bistro and your goal is to choose the best tomato paste for your spaghetti sauce, you prioritize your subset of properties, identify where each product falls in the pattern class, and then begin looking for patterns in the data/information.

**Pattern class:** Tomato paste

**Relevant properties:** Taste, color, texture, smell, and price

TABLE 5.1  **Pattern Class:** Preference for Local Organic Tomato Sauce

| Brand | Taste | Color | Texture | Smell | Price ($) |
|---|---|---|---|---|---|
| Local Organic1 | 4 | 3 | 2 | 4 | 2.01 |
| Local Organic2 | 3 | 4 | 3 | 3 | 1.98 |
| National Brand1 | 2 | 2 | 3 | 2 | 1.49 |
| National Brand2 | 2 | 2 | 2 | 4 | 1.75 |

**Pattern indicates:** A preference for local organic tomato sauce

People construct their own "abstractions of reality" on the basis of information available to them, but the perception of this input is affected by our personal mental processes that determine which information is included, how it is organized, and the weight attributed to it. What people perceive, how readily they perceive it, and how they process this information after receiving it are all strongly influenced by past experience, education, cultural values, role requirements, and organizational norms, as well as by the specifics of the information received.

The consequence of this process is that we all live in a very different world from one another. It is very difficult (perhaps impossible) for one person to see the same thing as another. We may both say that we see a can of tomato paste, but *pattern classes* for tomato paste are different. Differences in abstractions cause differences in conclusions.

If the role of the decision maker in the previous example were to be changed to supermarket owner, the analysis might look more like this:

**Pattern class:** Tomato paste

**Relevant properties:** Shelf life, brand recognition, availability, price margin, and cost

TABLE 5.2 **Pattern Classes:** Preference for National Brand-Name Tomato Sauce

| Brand | Shelf Life | Brand Recognition | Availability | Price Margin | Cost ($) |
|---|---|---|---|---|---|
| Local Organic1 | 2 | 1 | 1 | 1 | 1.98 |
| Local Organic2 | 3 | 1 | 1 | 2 | 1.99 |
| National Brand1 | 4 | 4 | 3 | 4 | 1.15 |
| National Brand2 | 4 | 3 | 4 | 3 | 1.25 |

**Pattern indicates:** A preference for national brand-name tomato sauce

Both the bistro owner and the supermarket owner were analyzing tomato paste, but they were working from different **layers of abstraction**. Because their goals for tomato paste were so different, they chose different relevant details to examine and probably arrived at different conclusions.

Because human mental capacity is finite, the mind cannot cope directly with the complexity of the world. Using abstraction, we construct simplified mental models of reality and then work with these models. Although layers of abstraction provide powerful tools for making complex systems, information, and processes more workable, they must be used carefully.

> **Fallacy: A kind of argument that tends to persuade us, even though it is a bad argument, either because of the form or because of the falsity of one of the premises.**

## Layers of Abstraction

Because abstractions are such powerful tools, it comes as little surprise that they are often either accidentally or purposefully used to misinform and mislead. A fallacy is, very generally, an error in reasoning. This differs from a factual error, which is simply being wrong about the facts. Here are three classic patterns of fallacy that lead to flawed abstractions: the false dilemma, the slippery slope, and the straw man fallacy.

### The False Dilemma

The false dilemma fallacy is based on a flawed or overly simplistic interpretation of the goals and/or available options. Putting issues or opinions into black-or-white terms is a common instance of this fallacy. This is how the false dilemma pattern works:

1. Someone claims that either X is true or Y is true (X and Y could both be false).

2. Then they claim that Y is false.

3. Therefore claim X *must* be true.

This line of reasoning is often incorrect because if both claims could be false, then it cannot be inferred that one is true because the other is false. Here's an example:

1. Either $2 + 2 = 5$ or $3 + 3 = 5$
2. It is not the case that $2 + 2 = 5$
3. Therefore $3 + 3 = 5$

The false dilemma pattern often points in the wrong direction because it artificially limits the available options.

*"You have two choices: either you declare bankruptcy now or you purchase our company's new product and save your firm."*

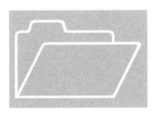

### Case Study: We Need It Yesterday!

"If we do not purchase XYZ's oxidizer for removing hazardous fumes from our plant's emissions, the EPA's fines will force us into bankruptcy," stated the senior safety and health officer of a small manufacturing company. "But what about its efficiency?" asked the chief financial officer. "Efficiency is not the issue. Getting a system in place quickly will save our company," again argued the safety and health officer.

Faced with the common problem of procrastination, a company found itself facing a false dilemma. We are often asked to make quick decisions without analyzing the long-term effects and cost of ownership. Would the company be forced into bankruptcy if a 30-day study were completed on oxidizer equipment? Why was the oxidizer company pushing for fast implementation?

A later analysis of the company's weak financial condition revealed that the natural gas used by the unit purchased from the quick-to-implement XYZ Company used 10 times the natural gas used by newer systems. The cost of ownership was bankrupting the company.

When faced with business decisions that appear to require immediate decisions, beware and be wise. Do not be deceived by false dilemmas and limited abstractions.

### The Slippery Slope (Also Known as the Camel's Nose)

In the slippery slope fallacy, a person asserts that some event must inevitably follow another without any argument for the inevitability of the event in question. Typically, the presenter follows a series of steps or gradations between one event and the one in question, and no reason is given as to why the intervening steps or gradations will simply be bypassed. This argument has the following form:

1. Event X has occurred (or will or might occur).
2. Therefore Event Y will inevitably happen.

This sort of logic is usually flawed because there is no reason to believe that one event must inevitably follow from another without presenting a case for such a claim. By increasing the number of steps, you will increase the likelihood that the logic will fail. Here are a few examples:

*"Our government shouldn't send troops into other countries. Once we send in our troops, we will end up in another Vietnam."*

*"The camel whose nose is in the tent tonight will be all the way in a few nights hence."*

## The Straw Man Fallacy

When the straw man argument is used, one party simply ignores the other party's actual abstraction and substitutes a distorted, exaggerated, or misrepresented version of that position. This straw man fallacy has the following pattern:

1. Person A has position X.
2. Person B presents position Y (which is a distorted version of X).
3. Person B attacks position Y.
4. Therefore position X is false.

Person A attacks an abstraction, which is different from, and usually weaker than, the opposition's best abstraction.

*"My opponent believes that higher taxes are the only way to pay for needed improvements. He never met a tax he didn't like. But I have a better idea: Let's not simply throw money at this issue."*

One person's account of the statements or views of another is not always a case of a straw man fallacy. You can corroborate such an account in the same way you judge any authority or expert testimony: by who that authority is, by the apparent accuracy of the account, and—in the case of a straw man fallacy—by the likelihood that the person being discussed would agree, for the most part, with the description of his or her statements or views.

**Distraction fallacies:** The structure or wording of an argument distracts us from being aware of some important and relevant facts, which makes the argument less plausible. False dilemma, slippery slope, and straw man all represent distraction fallacies.

All humans perceive reality differently, based on the unique layers of abstraction that their minds create. These abstractions can be the catalyst for great leaps of innovation or painfully expensive miscalculations. Abstractions provide the filters that allow us to drink in the amazing expanse of human experience. The best tool to ensure that you are not led astray by a poorly formed abstraction is an honest and open dialogue. Greater diversity of individuals in the dialogue will lead to more ideas that are better filtered. This is why modern companies seek to leverage the combined intellectual capital of their employees, customers, and partners. A combined effort to reach common goals is called collaboration.

# Collaboration

> *Education is a kind of continuing dialog, and a dialog assumes different points of view.*
>
> —Robert M Hutchins, Chancellor, University of Chicago, on academic freedom, *Time*, December 8, 1952
>
> *Without friendship and the openness and trust that go with it, skills are barren and knowledge may become an unguided missile.*
>
> —Frank H.T. Rhodes, Commencement address at Cornell University, May 29, 1983

Collaboration is not about debate or discussion—it is about dialogue. The paradox of collaboration is that through the process of interacting with others, individuals discover more of themselves. This is because collaboration often uncovers ideas that we find alien or threatening. These ideas are often the very ideas we have denied or repressed within ourselves. We need those ideas!

The goal of debating is to win an argument. Dialogue, however, is about working toward a common goal and expanding our current thinking. Dialogue is also different from discussion. To collaborate, you have to be willing to listen to what others are saying and allow yourself to be influenced by it. Anything less is merely empty discussion.

## Five Requirements for Successful Collaboration

1. *Dialogue.* Collaboration can only exist in the presence of dialogue. If you try building relationships without having an understanding of your potential partners and their unique perspectives, you will probably succeed in building a negative relationship. Dialogue typically strengthens personal relationships and solves problems, but it cannot be substituted with two monologues. The key difference between dialogue and empty discussion is valuing the points of view of others. A good understanding of the philosophy of KM should lead to an attitude that respects, values, and demands a diversity of viewpoints. In diversity, there is strength, adaptability, and insight.

2. *Trust.* Dialogue requires a certain degree of mutual trust. Collaboration among people of unequal status and authority can make dialogue more difficult to achieve. Avoid displaying coercive, authoritarian attitudes and flatten the political hierarchy to help build that trust. No project can be a complete failure for you if you can use it as an opportunity to improve your relationship with your co-workers. By the same token, no project can be a complete success if the price of success is bad relationships with your co-workers.

3. *Common goals.* Members of a collaboration team come to the table with their own agendas, fears, assumptions, and requirements. Expecting them to ignore these issues is both naïve and dangerous. Once an atmosphere of trust and two-way dialogue have been achieved, work toward making everyone's position clear and explicit. Too often collaboration means being dropped into a group of people you don't know to write a document

in which you have no interest or belief. This benefits no one. Strive for win-win scenarios in all of your business dealings.

4. *Empathy.* Discussion is more common than dialogue because people find it easy to express their opinions and exchange ideas with others, but they usually do not respond positively to opinions with which they disagree. Although it is easier to spend time congratulating people who agree with you, effective collaboration calls for finding common ground within the ideas of those with whom you disagree. Be ready to truly listen to others and to look for win-win solutions whenever possible.

5. *Openness.* Collaboration requires that participants be uninhibited in bringing their assumptions into the open, where others can respond to them. Unexamined assumptions typically result in misunderstandings and errors, so it is better to get the bad ideas on the table than to squash them. Openness ensures that your collaboration strategy does not rely on false assumptions of shared goals and diverging abstractions among participants. Also, today's bad idea can often become tomorrow's innovative solution.

Your communication style is important for supporting your collaboration efforts.

## Three Critical Collaboration Skills to Develop

- ❑ Effective and well-formatted communications
- ❑ Effective listening
- ❑ Effective strategies for conflict resolution

## Effective and Well-formatted Communications

Drafting effective communications is a key task for all knowledge workers. Don't overlook the importance of grammar, spelling, and formatting in your communications. Writing any document, even an e-mail, is an investment that should be taken seriously. Documents have costs, such as the following:

- ❑ It costs you time to write and review documents.
- ❑ It costs you money to publish documents in almost any format.
- ❑ It costs you opportunities if documents fail to make their point.
- ❑ It costs you credibility to represent your company, project, or brand poorly.

Good documentation is your friend because it will almost always improve a process. There is a perception that documents obstruct progress, and that can be true, if the documents are unclear; however, documentation created with the proper structure and discipline almost always leads to new insights. Accelerating action in your processes requires capturing ideas and making them understood; effective documentation makes this happen.

Moving to an information-based economy is increasing the incentive for people to hoard knowledge—just as the materials-based economy often rewarded people for hoarding goods. While individual competence is vital, it should be increasingly measured in a group context. High performers who are unwilling to help transfer their skills to other team members may be doing more harm than good. We need to change how we measure success both in the business and the academic world. Without this cultural change, people will continue to be rewarded for noncollaborative behaviors, rather than being encouraged to collaborate in building knowledgebases.

## Effective Listening

Effective collaboration requires far more than merely issuing an invitation to participate. Leaders and participants need to be willing to change their perspectives and to listen to one another with a positive and responsive attitude. Listening assumes an active involvement in the interaction taking place, and not just passively hearing sounds.

> **Empathy: Identification with and understanding of another's situation, feelings, and motives.**

Most effective listening techniques are based on empathy.

> *People only listen when they feel listened to.*
> —Carl Rogers

## Three Key Advantages of Reflective Listening

Reflection is a listening technique common in consulting work and psychological therapy. It seeks to keep a conversation moving without providing judgments regarding what is being discussed. In reflection, the listener clarifies and restates what the other person is saying, which provides three key advantages:

1. It can increase the listener's understanding of the other person.

2. It can help the other person to clarify his or her thoughts.

3. It can reassure the other person that someone is willing to attend to his or her point of view and wants to help.

People are more productive when their ideas are listened to and acted upon. They will go the extra mile when their feelings are validated. The question "Why?" can be surprisingly damaging because it defies the other person to find a justification or logical explanation that is acceptable to the helper. It implies a basic lack of trust that may or may not be present. Instead, try saying: "That's interesting. Can you tell me more about it?"

Reflective listening is

1. Asking open-ended questions and evaluating the message objectively

2. Maintaining positive body language throughout the discussion

3. Using supportive statements (e.g., "I see," "that's interesting")

4. Paraphrasing what the other person has said (e.g., "So, if I understand you correctly, then . . .")

5. Summarizing and confirming your understanding of what you've heard

Listening is important. It is perhaps one of the least recognized and potentially most useful skills at your disposal. The fact is that people are badgered, harassed, lectured, and preached to so much these days that they long for the company of good listeners. Effective listening is your best tool for improving all of the five requirements for successful collaboration. Practice your listening techniques with everyone you meet. Effective listening will be as beneficial to you outside of the workplace as inside.

## Effective Strategies for Conflict Resolution

Conflict is endemic in any organization, but when properly managed, conflict is more likely to be healthy than harmful. Wherever different choices exist, there is potential for disagreement. Conflict situations, when handled properly, can result in richer, more effective, creative solutions and interactions. When handled improperly, differences lead to confrontations and intransigence. Learning to disagree amicably and work through problems is one of the most important communication skills we can develop.

> **Conflict resolution: Problem-solving techniques in which the parties in dispute express their points of view, voice their interests, and find mutually acceptable solutions.**

Many books have been written on the subject of conflict resolution, and there will certainly be many more to come. From the squabbles of toddlers to nations at war, there is no shortage of need for people skilled in the delicate art of conflict resolution. Although we can only scratch the surface in this text, there are a few key conflict resolution ideas that we would like to introduce.

> *"A recent study found that 42% of a manager's time is spent on reaching agreement with others when conflicts occur."*
>
> —C. Watson and R. Hoffman, "Managers as Negotiators," *Leadership Quarterly* 7, 1996

## Set the Tone with Positive Responses

Some event is always the catalyst for conflict, but the end result is in the hands of the participants. How we respond to conflict can determine whether a conflict becomes focused on problem solving or focused on personal power struggles. Positive responses de-escalate the conflict. They reduce the tension and keep the conflict focused on ideas and problem solving. Negative responses make things worse; they do little to reduce the conflict and create an environment that is likely to be hostile to collaboration in the future.

"I messages" are less confrontational and less condescending than "you messages." Chances of getting compliance and cooperation increase with this approach to communication. The wording can initially be a bit cumbersome, but it becomes easier with practice. We can all benefit from improving our verbal responses. For example:

*"You weren't listening. You're going to end up dead or in jail."*

Could be rephrased into the following I message:

*"I want my sons to listen closely so that they can learn important things that will help them succeed in life."*

"I messages" let people know what you are thinking and feeling. They typically describe a behavior, its effects, and how it makes you feel. It feels kind of strange at first, but like reflective listening, it has surprising power both at the office and at home. I messages are much more productive and assertive responses than simply ignoring the problem or just expressing your anger or frustration.

Problem words that **escalate** a conflict are: *never, always, unless, can't, won't, don't, should,* and *shouldn't.*

Helpful words that **de-escalate** a conflict are: *maybe, perhaps, sometimes, what if, it seems like, I feel, I think,* and *I wonder.*

Your body language counts as a response in any situation. Positive body language helps to keep tempers cool and minds open to new ideas. Try to follow these guidelines:

- ❑ All parties should be either sitting or standing.
- ❑ Take a deep breath to stay relaxed.
- ❑ Look the other person in the eye.
- ❑ Speak softly and without haste.
- ❑ Keep your legs and arms uncrossed.
- ❑ Do not clench your fists or purse your lips.

## Speak the Same Language

People in conflict tend to focus on their positions, instead of focusing on their needs. These positions often come into conflict because of the differences in personal abstractions. The more diverse two parties' backgrounds are, the more they need to be able to communicate effectively. Sadly, the paradox is that their abstractions are so different that effective communication can be almost impossible. Exploring the significant language terms that hold different meanings for the parties involved in a conflict can often defuse a situation before it explodes. A larger abstraction of reality can sometimes accommodate the individual's threatened needs that are energizing the dispute.

## Why the Confusion?

According to the classic theory of Abraham Maslow, there are four types of needs that must be satisfied before a person can act unselfishly. Maslow called this the Hierarchy of Needs. In his theory, an individual's needs are arranged into a pyramid. Satisfying one set of needs at a time ascends the pyramid. Our most basic drives are physiologic. After that comes the need for safety, then the desire for love, and then for esteem. This was not exactly a shocking revelation.

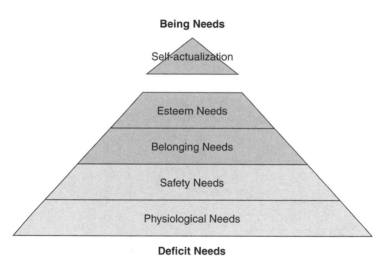

FIGURE 5.1 **Maslow's Hierarchy of Needs Pyramid.**

What made Maslow's idea unique is its concept of pre-potency. A pre-potent need is the one that has the greatest power or influence over our actions. It was Maslow's theory that everyone has a pre-potent need, but the need differs among individuals. In addition, an individual is not ready to express the higher-level needs until the lower-level needs have been met. A craving for love might motivate some people, whereas others may be motivated by a desire for esteem. A person's pre-potent need is the lowest unmet need in the pyramid.

Knowing where a person is on this scale can help determine what is motivating his or her behavior and hopefully help the two parties find common goals.

## Find Common Goals

❑ Really listen to what the other person is saying, with the goal of truly understanding that person's point of view.

❑ Affirm and acknowledge the other person's position.

❑ Ask questions that encourage the other person to look for a solution.

❑ Ask open-ended questions rather than ones that evoke a "yes" or "no" response.

❑ Keep looking for alternative ideas to resolve your dispute so that both of you have your needs met.

❑ Look for win-win scenarios.

### Dialogue

Because safety needs are lower in the hierarchy created by Abraham Maslow than needs for love and esteem, how is it possible that people might willingly die for love of their country?

### Additional Learning Resources

❑ www.datanation.com/fallacies/index.htm—The Logical Fallacies

❑ *The Wiki Way: Collaboration and Sharing on the Internet,* by Bo Leuf and Ward Cunningham (2001)

❑ *Infinite Wealth: A New World of Collaboration and Abundance in the Knowledge Era,* by Barry C. Carter (1999)

❑ *Native American Oral Traditions: Collaboration and Interpretation,* by Larry Evers (Editor), Barre Toelken (Editor), and John Miles Foley (2001)

❑ *How to Write Usable User Documentation,* by Edmond H. Weiss (1991)

❑ *Listening to Conflict: Finding Constructive Solutions to Workplace Disputes,* by Erik J. Van Slyke (1999)

❑ *Difficult Conversations: How to Discuss What Matters Most,* by Douglas Stone, Bruce Patton, Sheila Heen, and Roger Fisher (2000)

## Test Your Knowledge

## Discussion Questions

1. For data to become information, it requires what two things?

2. How do humans analyze information?

3. How does your past affect your opinions?

4. How does a computer solve problems?

5. How is your perception of something formed?

6. Can someone else have the exact same perception of something as you? Why?

7. Is the human mental capacity finite or infinite?

8. Have you ever believed that something was true because what seemed its opposite was false?

9. Can you learn about yourself by listening to someone else describe themselves?

10. What is required for effective collaboration?

## Review Questions

1. Most knowledge workers spend their time involved in _____ recognition.

2. We use layers of _____ to make these patterns more visible.

3. Effective knowledge workers draw on their _____ of abstractions to find new insights and opportunities in the available information and data patterns.

4. As social structures grew and increased in complexity, another layer of abstraction was added:_____.

5. One can enjoy talking on the phone without knowing how to _____ a telephone.

6. It is essentially an act of _____, ignoring or hiding details to capture the commonalities between different instances.

7. Conversely, a _____ can detect and recognize complex patterns with only a minimal amount of training.

8. Because abstractions are such powerful tools, it comes as little surprise that they are often either accidentally or purposefully used to _____ and _____.

9. The _____ _____ fallacy is based on a flawed or overly simplistic interpretation of the goals and/or available options.

10. The false dilemma pattern often points in the wrong direction because it _____ limits the available options.

11. When the _____ _____ argument is used, one party simply ignores the other party's actual abstraction and substitutes a distorted, exaggerated, or misrepresented version of that position.

12. All humans _____ _____ differently, based on the unique layers of abstraction that their minds create.

13. The best tool to ensure that you are not led astray by a poorly formed abstraction is an _____ and _____ dialogue.

14. The paradox of _____ is that through the process of interacting with others, individuals discover more of themselves.

15. _____ is about working toward a common goal and expanding our current thinking.

16. Good _____ is your friend because it will almost always improve a process.

17. Moving to an information-based economy is increasing the incentive for people to _____ _____, just as the materials-based economy often rewarded people for hoarding goods.

18. High _____ who are unwilling to help transfer their skills to other team members may be doing more harm than good.

19. Leaders and participants need to be willing to change their perspectives and to _____ to one another with a positive and responsive attitude.

20. Conflict situations, when handled properly, can result in richer, more effective, creative _____ and _____.

21. People in conflict tend to focus on their _____, instead of focusing on their needs.

22. According to the classic theory of Abraham Maslow, there are four types of _____ that must be satisfied before a person can act unselfishly.

## Chapter Vocabulary

**Abstraction:** Process of leaving out of consideration one or more properties of a complex issue so as to attend to others.

**Collaboration:** The act of working jointly.

**Conflict resolution:** Problem-solving technique in which the parties in dispute express their points of view, voice their interests, and find mutually acceptable solutions.

**Dialogue:** An informal exchange of views.

**Distraction fallacy:** An argument structured or worded in a way that distracts from the most important and relevant facts.

**Empathy:** Identification with and understanding of another's situation, feelings, and motives.

**Fallacy:** A kind of argument that tends to persuade us, even though it is a bad argument, either because of the form or because of the falsity of one of the premises.

**Maslow's pyramid:** Classic theory of Abraham Maslow stating that there are four types of needs that must be satisfied before a person can act unselfishly and reach self-actualization: physiological needs, safety needs, belonging needs, and esteem needs.

**Pattern class:** Elements that make up and describe which specific characteristics define a particular abstraction.

**Pattern recognition:** Identification of objects and images by their shapes, forms, outlines, color, surface texture, temperature, or other attributes.

**Reflective listening:** Paraphrasing to understand another person's meaning in a dialogue; allowing the other person to clarify his or her intent and correct any misinterpretations.

**The camel's nose:** See also *the slippery slope.*

**The false dilemma:** Deceptive logic based on a flawed or overly simplistic interpretation of the goals and/or available options.

**The slippery slope:** Deceptive logic that asserts that some event must inevitably follow from another (aka: the camel's nose).

**The straw man fallacy:** Deceptive logic that substitutes a distorted, exaggerated, or misrepresented version of the opposing position.

# Storytelling and Knowledge Transfer

*One way to help a company retain its vibrancy, even if its essential business appears to be mundane and repetitive, is to look for the drama in the everyday actions of people and celebrate it through the sharing of stories. In small ways, each of us can frame our work in heroic terms. Just as a good author can find a story where others see only the commonplace deeds of ordinary people, leaders of companies can help their employees live the heroic journey by providing challenges that draw upon their will to succeed in the face of difficulty.*

—Richard Stone, President of the StoryWork Institute

*Stories exist in all organizations and are an integral part of defining what that organization is and what it means to work for it.*

—Dave Snowden, Director of IBM's Institute for Knowledge Management

## Chapter Six Learning Objectives

- ❑ See what makes explicit knowledge easier to capture and share but less valuable than tacit knowledge.
- ❑ Learn to use stories to illustrate extremely complicated concepts in brief, memorable, and easily repeated ways.
- ❑ Make your communications more convincing, contextual, and compelling through storytelling.
- ❑ See why well-crafted stories are self-propagating.

It is widely accepted that there are two classes of knowledge: explicit and tacit. Explicit knowledge is often the only knowledge that is visible, so it is tempting to focus on it, but we know that most of our valuable knowledge is tacit. Because of the complexity of work today, knowledge workers inevitably find great difficulties in communicating complicated ideas through abstract forms of communication.

Explicit knowledge is knowledge that is definable and objective. Therefore, it can be easily documented and transferred. Tacit knowledge lives in an individual's head and in his or her behaviors. It's the subjective, context-rich knowledge that hides from people's consciousness even though they use it daily. Tacit knowledge is the most valuable type of knowledge we possess, but it can be difficult to transfer. You have probably known someone in your life who was an excellent speller. Chances are that person can't tell you *how* he or she recognizes a misspelled word—it just "doesn't look right." In business and in life, some decision-making processes are tacit and not easily distilled into explicit rules.

Analytic, abstract thinking is ideal for delivering messages concerning routinely observable things. By contrast, **narrative thinking** or **storytelling** enables us to imagine new perspectives and is ideally suited to communicating change, promoting values, and stimulating innovation. It offers the ability to illustrate extremely complicated concepts in a brief, memorable, and easily repeated way. Storytelling can be a powerful tool in the arsenal of any agent of organizational change.

The word *narration* comes from the Latin word *narrere*, and it means "to pass on knowledge." The following story illustrates one of the unique benefits of this KM tool.

### Case Study: Storytelling for Business

A certain grocery store chain needed to improve its employees' customer service skills. Formal corporate communications methods, such as meetings, had been tried in the past, with the usual results. Hoping to make a change, the company decided to try storytelling as a corporate communications tool.

Working with KM consultants from IBM Global Services, the company chose to retell a story about a customer who had dropped her grocery bags on the ground after checking out. The story described an employee's response that got him a reward for extraordinary customer service. The thing that truly makes this story special is the novel approach that management took to disseminating the story: word of mouth.

At noon on a Wednesday, one employee shared this story at a water cooler in another retail location. In only two days, the story had been heard at 600 "listening posts" throughout the organization, in six countries and in three languages. The story circulated by phone, fax, and e-mail as well as word of mouth. Good stories have their own momentum. A company just needs to listen for inspiring company tales, develop the seed stories, and start them circulating.

### The Two Software Companies

There once were two fiercely competing software companies, both of which made very high-quality applications. They constantly had new customers calling on them; however, one software company became wealthy and powerful while the other company, despite very hard work, became increasingly poor and exhausted. Finally, its rival consumed the less prosperous company.

The applications that the software makers created consisted of huge amounts of extremely complicated code. One company's development process was designed such that, when any developer made significant changes to a piece of the application, the partially completed program immediately gained new bugs and rework was slow to complete because of confusion and infighting. Trying desperately to keep the growing enterprise profitable, the company hired scores of programmers to help with the workload, but they found the labor tedious and soon left to find fortunes elsewhere.

The other, more successful software company designed its development process differently. Developers put together much simpler individual component modules. These modules could be put together to make larger program modules. Finally, several of the large modules made up a whole application. With this system, each module could be improved, tested, and validated separately, without creating problems for existing components. They also found that training workers was easier because the workers could learn one component at a time. Their improved process allowed them to consume their rival as well as create a strong business that continues to this day.

### Lessons of the Story

- ❏ For complex systems, develop encapsulated subprocesses to ensure that the systems survive disturbances gracefully, reduce rework required, and support incremental evolution.
- ❏ Large, complex systems invariably have a hierarchical structure.
- ❏ Quality, hard work, and dedication can be trumped by the power of technological innovation. Don't just work harder, work smarter.
- ❏ Subprocesses, like layers of abstraction, reduce the perceived complexity of large systems.

After reading both the story and the list of lessons from the story, which did you find more compelling and memorable?

## Storytelling: The Ancient Art of KM

> *Words convey the mental treasures of one period to the generations that follow; and laden with this, their precious freight, they sail safely across gulfs of time in which empires have suffered shipwreck and the languages of common life have sunk into oblivion.*
>
> —Anonymous

Think about your childhood, when your parents read you stories. Did your parents have an objective in telling you the story? Consider classic children's tales like David and Goliath, The Tortoise and the Hare, or The Gingerbread Man. Typically, the story teaches several lessons and morals. In addition to teaching the lesson, the story inspires the child to behave in a certain way. It is also worth noting that the moral of the story adds credibility to the details.

### Key Advantages of Storytelling

- ❑ People tend to hear stories in a receptive mode rather than a defensive mode.
- ❑ Abstract arguments are often combative in nature.
- ❑ Stories are usually more memorable than other forms of communication.
- ❑ Stories focus on what instinctively matters to people.
- ❑ Stories are not so bound by logic; they thrive on conflict, surprises, and change.
- ❑ Stories can unleash a spirit of heroism.
- ❑ Stories help workers frame their work in loftier and more significant terms.

Storytelling is central to the expression of the human condition. Stories have always been used to exchange and propagate complex ideas, influence action, and inspire creativity. More authentic, more convincing, and more involving than lecture, debate, or abstract logic, stories thrive on conflict, surprises, and change. Today, businesses are beginning to realize the potential impact of storytelling within their organizations. There are several strong uses for storytelling within your company:

- ❑ Promoting organizational change
- ❑ Delivering communications
- ❑ Capturing tacit knowledge
- ❑ Transferring tacit knowledge
- ❑ Spurring innovation
- ❑ Building community

The two main types of stories useful in KM are what we'll call *business fables* and *business anecdotes*.

**Business fables**: Fictitious narrations intended to reveal some useful value, idea, or precept.

**Business anecdotes**: True narrations intended to reveal some useful value, idea, or precept.

Both types of stories can be compelling tools for business, but business anecdotes are typically the strongest tool for influencing behavior.

### Case Study: 3M

3M, founded early in the twentieth century, was a mining company. Since their mining days, 3M has come a long way. The company's researchers and developers have created a multitude of new technologies. These technologies have become the foundation for more than 50,000 innovative products. 3M accomplished this by encouraging creativity and expecting innovation from its employees. The company's researchers can spend up to 15% of their time on any project that interests them.

This leeway has created massive benefits to the employees and to 3M. One catalyst for innovation 3M uses is storytelling.

Here's an example:

### The Glue That Wouldn't Stick

Art Fry, a new-product development researcher for 3M, dealt with a small irritation every Sunday morning as he sang in the church choir. After marking his pages in the hymnal with small bits of paper, the small pieces would invariably fall out all over the floor. Like many practically minded leaders, however, Art Fry recognized problems as opportunities in waiting.

In 1968, 3M research scientist Dr. Spence Silver developed an adhesive that would not dissolve, could not be melted, and did not stick very strongly when coated onto tape backings. Conventional wisdom held that it was a uniquely awful adhesive for tape because it did not stick very well, but Silver would not be discouraged. For five years Silver gave seminars within 3M advocating his unique new adhesive. One of the attendees happened to be Art Fry, and he was intrigued by the properties of Dr. Silver's creation.

One day, Fry realized that Silver's adhesive could be used for a wonderfully reliable bookmark. Fry coated the adhesive on a paper sample and found that it was not only a good bookmark, but it was also great for writing notes. It would stay in place as long as you wanted it to, and then you could remove it without damaging the note or any paper it was attached to. A whole new concept for communicating, organizing, and reminding was about to be born.

Art Fry's out-of-the-box thinking, combined with 3M's knowledge-valuing strategy, proved to be a real moneymaker. The resulting product was called Post-it® and has become one of 3M's most successful office products. By valuing ideas—even bad ideas—3M created a product that permanently changed the way we communicate. In fact, there are now more than 400 Post-it products sold in more than 100 countries around the world. They come in 27 sizes, 56 shapes, and 50 colors.

### Lessons of the Story

❑ True wisdom is rarely conventional.

❑ Don't discard bad ideas because they are often valuable when applied to a different context.

❑ Collaboration is your best bet for finding a new context for an existing idea.

❑ Problems always contain hidden opportunities to those with the imagination to find them.

Today's companies are realizing that storytelling is an unavoidable force within communities. Like children with inappropriate toys, it can be tough to stop employees from telling stories of company screwups and bureaucracy. Redirecting them toward more positive behavior is usually much more effective. The Post-it Note is now one of the best known of all 3M products, and the story of its creation continues to inspire 3M employees to this day.

# Major Elements of KM Storytelling

*It's interesting to note, that every time an effective new storytelling technology has been introduced, it has changed our world. Examples include language, writing, the telegraph and telephone, newspapers, radio, television, and most recently, the Internet.*

—Bran Ferren, CEO of Applied Minds, Inc.

Storytelling is probably the oldest KM technique in existence. As a tool to teach lessons, change behaviors, and build community, it is unmatched in both power and ubiquity. Storytelling has been used by every culture in the world and throughout history because it calls on all of our senses and engages the whole of our brains. Our left brain's functions of logic, words, rational thought, and mathematics are balanced by the right brain's strengths of creativity, intuition, and emotion.

From ancient parables to modern-day fairy tales, you can expect any story to have a beginning, middle, and end. These three story sections typically serve the following purposes:

**The beginning:** Introduces the protagonist and his or her goals

**The middle:** Introduces a journey (crisis/opportunity) and the choices it demands

**The end:** Communicates the results of the choices made and their consequences

## The Hero's Journey Archetype

In 1949, a man named Joseph Campbell (1907–1987) wrote *The Hero with a Thousand Faces*. Campbell had discovered a story structure that seemed ubiquitous in many culture's mythologies. He called this a *monomyth*, but Carl Jung would have called it an archetype. Campbell had looked at cultural traditions all over the world, and there was always the same underlying structure, main points, and types of characters.

Campbell had thought that this similarity came from ancient humans' similar experiences in nomadic tribes. Your tribe might be doing fine, and then encounter a crisis, such as running out of water. Someone would have to be selected to go out and deal with it. This was the hero. Once out on the adventure, the hero would encounter many crises, trials, and adventures and then return with the solutions to the problem. This cycle has been termed "the hero's journey."

**Archetype: The original pattern or the model from which a thing is made or formed.**

The story of the journey originated in ancient myths and legends, and it is still in use today. It can be seen in almost all of the books, movies, and plays we read. First, the hero faces separation from his or her old, familiar world. A process of initiation and transformation then follows, brought on by a crisis and the choices the hero makes. Once the hero realizes the consequences of the choice, he or she returns home more confident, more perceptive, and more capable. An example of the hero's journey is presented in the following parable.

## The Parable of the Prodigal Son

There was a man who had two sons. The younger one said to his father, "Father, give me my share of the estate." So he divided his property between them. Not long after that, the younger son got together all he had, set off for a distant country, and there squandered his wealth in wild living.

After he had spent everything, there was a severe famine in that whole country, and the younger son began to be in need. So he went and hired himself out to a citizen of that country, who sent him to his fields to feed pigs. He longed to fill his stomach with the pods that the pigs were eating, but no one gave him anything. When he came to his senses, he said, "How many of my father's hired men have food to spare, and here I am starving to death! I will set out and go back to my father and say to him: 'Father, I have sinned against heaven and against you. I am no longer worthy to be called your son; make me like one of your hired men." So he got up and went to his father.

But while he was still a long way off, his father saw him and was filled with compassion for him; he ran to his younger son, threw his arms around him, and kissed him. The son said to him, "Father, I have sinned against heaven and against you. I am no longer worthy to be called your son." But the father said to his servants, "Quick! Bring the best robe and put it on him. Put a ring on his finger and sandals on his feet. Bring the fattened calf and kill it. Let's have a feast and celebrate. For this son of mine was dead and is alive again; he was lost and is found." So they began to celebrate.

Meanwhile, the older son was in the field. When he came near the house, he heard music and dancing. So he called one of the servants and asked him what was going on. "Your brother has come," he replied, "and your father has killed the fattened calf because he has him back safe and sound." The older son became angry and refused to go in. So his father went out and pleaded with him. But the older son answered his father, "Look! All of these years I've been slaving for you and never disobeyed your orders. Yet you never gave me even a young goat so I could celebrate with my friends. But when this son of yours who has squandered your property with prostitutes comes home, you kill the fattened calf for him!" "My son," the father said, "you are always with me, and everything I have is yours. But we had to celebrate and be glad, because this brother of yours was dead and is alive again; he was lost and is found."—Luke 15:11-32

### Lessons of the Story

❑ Some actions, which seem very attractive at first, lead to destruction.

❑ Progress requires acknowledging mistakes and making the decision to change.

❑ Sometimes children have to be allowed to learn from their own mistakes.

❑ Understanding and compassion lead to the preservation of the relationships we value most, not lectures or jealousy.

Although not typically considered a tale of heroism, the prodigal son story follows the traditional form of the hero's journey.

### The Structure of the Hero's Journey Archetype

There are seven key pieces of the hero's journey archetype. You can use this structure to add strength and resonance to your corporate stories.

1. **The intro:** The hero's world is introduced.
2. **The quest:** The hero finds or defines the problem.
3. **The departure:** The hero sacrifices his status quo.
4. **The confrontation:** The hero encounters tests, enemies, and allies.
5. **The struggle:** The hero struggles, usually with him- or herself, and hits bottom.
6. **The redemption:** The hero finds the answer, usually within him- or herself.
7. **The return:** The hero returns home with new knowledge and strength.

Knowledge is more easily transferred between individuals using stories for many reasons: (1) the listener becomes connected not only to the content, but also to the teller and to the process of the story unfolding; (2) the context, a component of information that is too often lost, is inherent in the way in which the story is related, which is a key objective in transferring tacit knowledge; and (3) knowledge transferred through storytelling more often leads to changes in behavior because it is a less confrontational form of communication.

### Dialogue

Stories are obviously a very powerful way to exchange knowledge and information. Can you think of any reasons why it might be unwise to rely on stories as the only source of information?

### Additional Learning Resources

❑ www.storytellingcenter.com/resources/articles/simmons.htm—The Six Stories You Need to Know How to Tell

❑ *The Story Factor: Inspiration, Influence, and Persuasion Through the Art of Storytelling*, by Annette Simmons (2002)

❑ *The Springboard: How Storytelling Ignites Action in Knowledge-Era Organizations*, by Stephen Denning (2000)

❑ *Shadows of the Neanderthal: Illuminating the Beliefs That Limit Our Organizations*, by David Hutchens and Bobby Gombert (1999)

❑ *The Power of Myth*, by Joseph Campbell, Bill Moyers, and Betty Sue Flowers (1991)

❑ *The Hero with a Thousand Faces*, by Joseph Campbell (1972)

## Test Your Knowledge

### Discussion Questions

1. How do you transfer knowledge?

2. Have you ever told a story to pass on information or a truth?

3. Do you believe that storytelling fits into business today?

4. How are stories structured?

5. How does the story pass on knowledge?

### Review Questions

1. It is widely accepted that there are two classes of knowledge: _____ and _____.

2. Explicit knowledge is knowledge that is _____ and _____ _____.

3. _____ knowledge lives in an individual's head and in his or her behaviors.

4. Analytic, abstract thinking is ideal for delivering messages concerning _____ observable things.

5. The word _____ comes from the Latin word *narrere*, and it means "to pass on knowledge."

6. Typically, the story teaches several lessons and _____.

7. Storytelling is central to the expression of the _____
   _____.

8. 3M, founded early in the 20th century, was a _____ company.

9. One catalyst for _____ 3M uses is storytelling.

10. Today's companies are realizing that _____ is an unavoidable
    force within communities.

11. Storytelling is probably the oldest _____ technique in existence.

12. From ancient parables to modern-day fairy tales, you can expect any story to have
    a _____, _____, and _____.

13. In 1949, a man named _____ _____ (1907–1987)
    wrote *The Hero with a Thousand Faces*.

14. The story of the _____ originated in ancient myths and legends
    and is still in use today.

## Chapter Vocabulary

**Archetype:** The original pattern or the model from which a thing is made or formed.

**Business anecdotes:** True narrations intended to reveal some useful value, idea, or precept.

**Business fables:** Fictitious narrations intended to reveal some useful value, idea, or precept.

**Encapsulation:** Providing a limited set of functions while hiding the internal workings of an operation.

**Explicit knowledge:** Knowledge that is captured in explicit, retrievable, easily shared form such as documents.

**Narrative thinking:** A mental model that is effective for finding causality, communicating change, promoting values, and stimulating innovation.

**Tacit knowledge:** Knowledge that lives in an individual's head and in his or her behaviors based on experiences.

**The hero's journey:** An archetype story where one leaves the world of his or her common life to undergo a journey where challenges and fears are overcome in order to secure a reward.

# Systems Thinking

*We learn best from our experience, but we never directly experience the consequences of many of our most important decisions.*

—Peter Senge, *The Fifth Discipline* (1990)

### Chapter Seven Learning Objectives

- ❑ Learn that complex systems are not linear in nature . . . they are circular.
- ❑ Understand that symptomatic solutions typically fail to address fundamental difficulties and result in cycles of reoccurring interventions.
- ❑ See how delays tend to increase the amount of oscillation in a system.
- ❑ Know that closed systems will fail as entropy inevitably builds up.
- ❑ Notice how buffers increase the ability of a system to adapt to changes in flow.

Mankind has succeeded over time in conquering the physical world largely by adopting the analytic method described earlier in this text. To understand problems, we break a problem into components, study each part in isolation, and then draw conclusions about the whole. This is a powerful technique for problem solving. Unfortunately, this sort of linear analysis is rarely effective in addressing large, complex organizational problems because complex systems are not linear in nature—they are circular.

## Circular vs. Linear Analysis

General systems theory was introduced in the 1940s by Ludwig von Berttalanffy and then was later expanded into the field of system dynamics in 1956 by MIT professor Jay Forrester. In 1990, Peter Senge released his widely acclaimed book, *The Fifth Discipline: The Art and Practice of the Learning Organization*. It sought to ameliorate the rapid advance of technologic complexities that have occurred in this century. It focused on the relationships and processes that make up complex systems (e.g., families, organizations, cities), rather than the separate entities or the sum of their parts. Since its publication, more than 750,000 copies of *The Fifth Discipline* have been sold, and it is still considered one of the most influential business books ever written.

Basically, the concept of systems thinking represents a way of helping a person view the world from a broader, less linear perspective that includes structures, patterns, events, and feedback rather than just the events. By identifying the true causes of problems within systems, we can then figure out how to address them. This approach is helpful in avoiding symptomatic solutions. Symptomatic solutions typically fail to address fundamental difficulties and result in cycles of recurring interventions.

## Example of a Symptomatic Solution

An automobile manufacturer notices a trend of decreasing sales in one of its lines of compact cars. The manufacturer responds by increasing advertising spending in its key market demographics. This logical step succeeds in increasing sales by 2% in the first two months of the fiscal quarter, but also results in a sales price increase for their cars. Unfortunately, by the end of the fiscal year, the compact car line sales statistics had dropped even further below the previous year's numbers. What could have brought this sales drop-off, in the face of increased advertising?

Increasing the amount of advertising addresses the *symptom* of lower sales, but if the *fundamental problem* is not a lack of consumer awareness, it may not be an effective solution. Consider the possibility that the lower sales could actually be caused by higher prices because the compact car market is very price sensitive. In that case, each jump in advertising spending might result in a short-term boost in sales but would inevitably be followed by a longer-term loss of its customer base.

## Causal Loop Diagrams

Systems thinkers do not simply focus on day-to-day events. They seek out the patterns and forces that enable or delay change. A basic term in systems thinking is *feedback*. In systems thinking, every influence is both a cause and an effect. One way of seeing problems systemically is to find circles of influence. By tracing the flow of influence, we can often see patterns, which repeat themselves, making situations better or worse. In systems thinking, we use **causal loops** to help visualize and communicate these influence flows. In most cases, feedback loops provide the major source of behavior and policy difficulties.

A *reinforcing loop* generates rapidly (often exponentially) accelerating growth and collapse. Change typically begins slowly but keeps speeding up as it reinforces itself. This snowballing effect generates what are normally called vicious circles or virtuous circles, depending on how they impact the bottom line for the business.

A reinforcing loop is typically confronted by a limiting effect or *balancing loop* (see Figure 7.1). A clockwise circle of arrows represents the reinforcing loop. Balancing loops typically limit growth and maintain the status quo. The counterclockwise circle of arrows represents the balancing loop. Each square or rectangle represents an action or a motivation that drives the behavior cycle.

Balancing processes are bound to targets, constraints, or goals that are often implicitly set by the forces of the system. Whenever the current system status fails to match the balancing

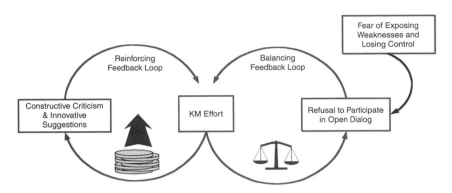

FIGURE 7.1 **Reinforcing Loops Generate Rapidly (Often Exponentially).** Note: Drawing based on techniques described in Peter Senge's book *The Fifth Discipline.*

loop's target, the resulting gap (between the target and the system's actual performance) generates pressure that the system cannot ignore. It's as if the system has a dedicated focus on "the right result" and will do whatever it takes to return to that state. Until you recognize the gap, and identify the goal or constraint that drives it, you cannot comprehend the behavior of the balancing loop.

A causal loop diagram may contain any combination of balancing and reinforcing loops. Peter Senge outlines some of these recurring causal loop patterns in *The Fifth Discipline.* He calls them system archetypes; by learning to identify these archetypes, we can recognize the feedback loops that cause them and where to find leverage.

## Leverage

Leverage represents positional advantage providing the power to act effectively. Senge uses the example of a rudder on a ship to explain the concept of leverage. A ship's rudder is tiny compared to the rest of a ship; nonetheless it hugely affects the behavior of the ship. Just a tiny amount of force applied to the rudder will completely change the direction of the ship. Yet, applying 100 times the force of the rudder at the helm of a ship, as opposed to its stern, provides absolutely no effect.

Points of leverage can be found in systems, processes, relationships, and so on, and choosing the right point of leverage often determines how successful an action will be. Choosing the right point of leverage gets the best results from small, well-focused actions, instead of from large, complex efforts. Unfortunately, we most often focus on the high-stress points in a system. This focus promotes reactive, symptom-based fixes that will have to be repeated over and over again.

## Feedback Delays

Delays represent another key issue in understanding the nature of feedback loops. Delays are increases in the length of time it takes for the characteristics of the structure to become observable. Delays tend to increase the amount of oscillation in a system. In causal diagrams, we represent delays with a pair of parallel lines. Here's an example:

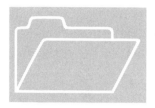

**Case Study: Feedback Delays**

A restaurant chain opened at a very attractive location in Tulsa, Oklahoma. The owners knew that the restaurant was meeting a real need, and they assumed that during peak meal times it would be filled almost up to its capacity with customers. That would make it a constant revenue generator; however, a few months after it opened, the number of customers leveled off. The restaurant started a community marketing campaign, and customer traffic rose for a time, but soon dropped off again.

Finally, the owners took a close look at their customer volume statistics. They spent time in the restaurant and surveyed staff at the front counter and customers. It turned out that when traffic was low, people were served quickly. Once the word got out that lines were short and quick at this restaurant, it once again became crowded. Because people have a natural distaste for waiting, they exercised their option to go elsewhere.

## The Subtle Impact of Delays

This problem was difficult to spot because of the feedback delays inherent in the process. There is a delay between the owner's *action* of increasing advertising and the resulting *observation* of customer traffic increases. There is also a delay between the customers' **observation** of reduced lines during slow restaurant traffic periods and their **action** of returning to the restaurant to eat.

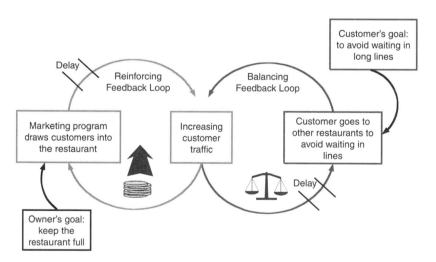

FIGURE 7.2 **Causal Loops Identifying Forces Limiting the Growth of Restaurant Customer Base.** Note: Drawing based on techniques described in Peter Senge's book *The Fifth Discipline.*

Delays can have a massive influence on a system's effectiveness; they often accentuate the impact of other forces. These feedback delays tend to disguise the dynamic complexity of a system. When the same action has dramatically different effects in the short and the long run, or when an action has one set of consequences locally and a different set of consequences in another part of the system, then there is dynamic complexity. Delays in dynamically complex systems can make you badly overshoot your goals or they can have a positive effect if you recognize them and work with them.

Delays are usually taken for granted, often ignored altogether, and almost always under-estimated. In reinforcing loops, delays affect customer and supplier confidence because action doesn't come as quickly as expected. In balancing loops, when delays occur, people tend to react impatiently, usually redoubling their efforts to get what they want. This results in unnecessarily volatile pendulum swings (oscillation) from one extreme to another. Also, delays are typically a source of waste; removing delays is a key method for speeding up cycle time. One of the purposes of drawing causal loop diagrams is to flag the delays, which you might otherwise miss.

Peter Senge describes the concept of oscillation by using the metaphor of adjusting the water temperature in a shower. The goal is to have a consistently comfortable water temperature in the shower. When some event (toilet flush) causes the water to suddenly become uncomfortably cold, the intuitive reaction is to quickly turn the hot water up much higher. After a short delay, the water then becomes painfully hot. This requires another adjustment to increase the amount of cold water again.

This pendulum will keep swinging from one extreme to another because of the delays between action and observed change and the tendency to overcompensate. The less intuitive solution would be to make no adjustment at all and wait for the system to normalize. Surprisingly, this lack of response will usually result in obtaining the objective faster. This is often described as "stock and flow" thinking.

## Stocks and Flows

A distinction must be made between variables that are measured at points in time and variables that represent totals or averages over an interval. Point-in-time values are often called stocks or levels. Variables that represent totals or averages over an interval are often called flows or rates.

- ❑ **Stocks** are accumulations; they're like checking account balances to which money is added or taken away.
- ❑ **Flows** are rates of change; they're like the schedule of deposits and withdrawals of money.

The federal *debt* represents the accumulation of all the deficits and surpluses over time. The federal debt is considered a stock. Stocks are accumulations; they're like buckets to which water is added or taken away.

The federal *deficit* occurs yearly. It represents the shortfall between money the government spends and money it receives in revenues. The federal deficit is considered a flow. Flows are what cause the stocks to change.

Stock and flow problems often result in oscillation within a system. When a system fluctuates between state of surplus and deficit (oscillation), the effects can be incredibly destructive. One possible leverage point for minimizing the negative impact of stock and flow fluctuation is through the use of buffers. By increasing the capacity of a system buffer, you can often improve the stability of a system. However, if the buffer is increased too much, the system becomes inflexible and loses agility.

> **System: A group of interacting, interrelated, and interdependent components that form a complex and unified whole.**

### Seeing the Big Picture with Systems Thinking

Each one of us plays many roles in life: child, parent, neighbor, voter, butcher, baker, candlestick maker, and so on, and each role brings its own set of changing relationships and abstractions. We exist in many different contexts, in many different systems. Knowledge of systems is a path to a better understanding of how businesses and human nature work. It helps us avoid escalating conflicts to dangerous levels by emphasizing the importance of such things as information flow, diversity, and openness.

One of the key concepts usually introduced in teaching systems thinking is the concept of open vs. closed systems. An open system exchanges information, material, or energy with its environment. Its outputs and outcomes affect and are influenced by the surrounding environment. As systems become more open they benefit from:

- ❏ A rich diversity of information resources to increase awareness
- ❏ Synergy among system components to improve agility
- ❏ Evolutionary improvement to ensure sustainability
- ❏ Competition to weed out the weak and obsolete components

**Synergy:** Originates from the Greek word *synergia*, which means "joint work and cooperative action." *Synergy* refers to the enhanced result of two or more components of a system working together (i.e., one plus one equals three). The ecosystem of our planet is considered a classic example of an open system; the inherent synergy of its components is the key to its long-term sustainability.

# Closed Systems vs. Open Systems

Closed systems are totally independent and considered to be somewhat isolated from environmental influences. The closed system accepts inputs from the environment and may deliver outputs into the environment, but there is no interaction during the transfer.

Closed systems will fail over time and inevitably fall into chaos because of the force of entropy, which is a universal tendency of all systems to disintegrate into randomness over time unless something counteracts this tendency. Closed systems are unable to obtain resources from the environment to combat the force of entropy. This limitation does not mean that closed systems are valueless, merely unsustainable over the long term. Here's an example:

A hydraulic system uses liquid under pressure to transmit energy. Hydraulic systems take engine power and convert it into hydraulic power by means of a sealed hydraulic pump. They can control motion without worrying about the effects of temperature and the weather. Hydraulic systems are closed systems; the atmosphere does not affect them. This provides consistent performance in a multitude of weather conditions, until the hardware wears out.

Open systems, because they have external sources of energy, information, or materials, are more agile. They are able to evolve into better systems, if they can utilize these inputs effectively. Information systems cannot be completely closed systems; they need information from the outside to achieve their purpose and produce information outputs that are useful to humans. Information systems that are more open are generally better because they are more responsive to their environment and because they are easier to connect to other external systems; however, there are limits to the degree of openness that can be tolerated.

Increased awareness of the strengths of open systems can help us recognize how we contribute to a larger system, and how we can collaborate in creating shared advantages. Some even consider closed systems to be the root cause of all human conflict. Rather than pursuing a goal of mutually shared benefits, one player pursues only what it perceives to be its own best interests, at the expense of the other, and win-win scenarios are never considered.

### Dialogue

Is the Earth a closed system or an open system?

Define what would make it the opposite system?

### Additional Learning Resources

- ❑ http://www.workteams.unt.edu/reports/bcooper.htm—*Systems Thinking: A Requirement for all Employees*, by Betty Cooper
- ❑ *How Systems Thinking/Systems Dynamics Helps to Identify Limits to Growth to Boost Innovation Value*, by Juergen Daum. The New Economy Analyst Report, October 6, 2001
- ❑ http://sysdyn.mit.edu/sdep/papers/D-4434-3.pdf—*Learning through System Dynamics as Preparation for the 21st Century*, by Jay Forrester (1994)
- ❑ *Business Dynamics: Systems Thinking and Modeling for a Complex World*, with CD-ROM, by John D. Sterman (2000)
- ❑ www.systemdynamics.org—The System Dynamics Society Homepage
- ❑ *Schools That Learn*, by Peter Senge et al. (2000)
- ❑ *Industrial Dynamics*, by Jay W. Forrester (1961)

 **Test Your Knowledge**

## Discussion Questions

1. How would you describe a bureaucracy? What makes it work?

2. Is there ever a good reason for bureaucracy?

3. Have you ever been baffled by a turn in events?

4. Are there patterns to events or are they completely random? Why?

5. How does the national debt influence the national deficit?

## Review Questions

1. To understand problems, we break a problem into _____, study each part in isolation, and then draw conclusions about the whole.

2. General systems theory was introduced in the 1940s by Ludwig von Berttalanffy and then was later expanded into the field of system dynamics in 1956 by MIT professor Jay _____.

3. Basically, the concept of _____ _____ represents a way of helping a person view the world from a broader, less linear perspective that includes structures, patterns, events, and feedback rather than just the events.

4. _____ solutions typically fail to address fundamental difficulties and result in cycles of recurring interventions.

5. _____ the amount of advertising addresses the *symptom* of lower sales, but if the *fundamental problem* is not a lack of consumer awareness, it may not be an effective solution.

6. In systems thinking, every influence is both a _____ and an effect.

7. In most cases, _____ loops provide the major source of behavior and policy difficulties.

8. A reinforcing loop is typically confronted by a limiting effect or _____ loop.

9. Balancing processes are bound to _____, _____, or _____ that are often implicitly set by the forces of the system.

10. Points of _____ can be found in systems, processes, relationships, and so on, and choosing the right point of leverage often determines how successful an action will be.

11. _____ represent another key issue in understanding the nature of feedback loops.

12. Delays are usually taken for granted, often ignored altogether, and almost always _____.

13. One of the purposes of drawing causal loop diagrams is to _____ the delays, which you might otherwise miss.

14. Point-in-time values are often called _____ or levels.

15. The federal debt represents the _____ of all the deficits and surpluses over time.

16. Stocks are accumulations; they're like _____ to which water is added or taken away.

17. _____ are what cause the stocks to change.

18. Knowledge of systems is a path to a _____ _____ of how businesses and human nature work.

19. Closed systems are totally _____ and considered to be somewhat isolated from environmental influences.

20. Open systems, because they have external sources of energy, information, or materials, are more _____.

## Chapter Vocabulary

**Accentuate:** To bring out distinctly, to prominently emphasize.

**Causal loop diagram:** Mental model used to analyze qualitative data where a network of variables is developed and the causal relationships between variables are explicitly delineated.

**Circular analysis:** A technique for analysis that focuses on the relationships and processes that make up complex systems (e.g., families, organizations, cities), rather than the separate entities or the sum of their parts.

**Closed systems:** Totally independent systems that are considered to be somewhat isolated from environmental influences.

**Flows:** Rates of change, similar to the schedule of deposits and withdrawals of money.

**Leverage:** Strategic positional advantage providing the power to act effectively.

**Linear analysis:** A technique for analysis where you break a problem into components, study each part in isolation, and then draw conclusions about the whole.

**Open systems:** Systems with external sources of energy, information, or materials.

**Oscillation:** Fluctuation, variation, changing back and forth.

**Qualitative analysis:** Analysis based on examining dynamic qualities and relationships holistically.

**Quantitative analysis:** Analysis based on the separate examination of the component parts of a subject.

**Stocks:** Accumulations; similar to checking accounts to which money is added or taken away.

**Symptomatic:** Pertaining to symptoms, happening in concurrence with something, indicating the existence of a larger problem.

**Synergy:** Joint work and cooperative action. Synergy refers to the enhanced result of two or more components of a system working together.

# Harnessing Metcalfe's Law: Utility = Nodes$^2$

*To capture knowledge you need two things: the enabling infrastructure must be in place, and you also need the right culture. Building the infrastructure is easy compared with building the right culture, and our organizations have not typically had cultures where these intangible qualities of information and knowledge have been nurtured and revered.*

—Clive Mather, CIO, Royal Dutch Shell

**Chapter Eight Learning Objectives**

❑ Know that the utility of a network is equal to the square of the number of nodes.

❑ Understand that experience, reflection, and sharing are the main ways that knowledge is increased.

❑ Demonstrate behaviors that value people and their needs.

❑ Learn to value attention and trust in your social network.

❑ Learn to recognize the four stages of team development.

The first part of this book focused on improving your bottom-line results by focusing on your personal information and knowledge management as strategic issues. Hopefully, by now you've come to some of the following conclusions:

❑ Our human ability to create unique abstractions empowers us to understand complex systems.

❑ Each of us uses different abstractions based on our own unique knowledge and experiences.

❑ This diversity of abstractions often causes communication problems, but can be a source for new insights and innovations.

The next part of this book will delve deeper into these issues. Creating a culture that values dialogue, knowledge sharing, and a diversity of ideas is your best bet for supporting innovation in your group. We will provide you with some common issues and some uncommon solutions to enable you to spread the technologies and philosophies of KM throughout your organization.

Knowledge flows very poorly in large, centralized, hierarchical, organizations. Companies get trapped in logjams of politics and personal power plays. In the typical corporate culture, it's believed that only senior management can find new innovations because only they can see the big picture. The simple fact is that no one sees the big picture. In fact, there is no one single big picture in any complex organization. Because we all use different abstractions to understand the complexities that surround us, we all have different pictures of the situation. Sadly, managers too often get stuck arguing about whose picture is the biggest instead of valuing plurality and learning from the wealth of diverse viewpoints.

Also, because many organizations measure each person on individual task performance, workers tend to look out for their own interests. Employees won't take the time to develop a new idea if their common tasks suffer in the meantime. This type of system often stalls the knowledge flow, and at times it stifles it completely.

Case studies of collaboration groups working within large corporations, such as Whirlpool, Eastman Kodak, and Hewlett-Packard, show that the effectiveness of a team is typically based on an underlying network of social relationships. Knowledge workers gain knowledge through direct experience and by reflecting on and sharing those experiences with others. If you want to make the individuals with whom you work part of a team that you can trust, you will need to provide business challenges that create opportunities to share ideas. Evaluate your people based on achieving group objectives, not simply on their individual goals.

One of the key duties for knowledge workers is offering fast and effective advice to meet business objectives, avoid risks, and seize new opportunities. In large organizations, you will never be able to advance these goals alone. You need a network.

## Managing a Workgroup KM Network

> The best information environments will take advantage of the ability of IT to overcome geography but will also acknowledge that the highest bandwidth network of all is found between the water fountain and the coffee machine.
>
> —T.H. Davenport, "Think Tank: The Virtual and the Physical," *CIO*, November 15, 1995

A workgroup represents any two or more individuals sharing information. Workgroups in corporations are formed both formally and informally to achieve business and personal goals. The alignment of the various personal and business goals of these individuals is the difference between a painful bureaucracy and a vibrant knowledge network.

Managing a successful workgroup KM network requires making sure that all of the major components of your network are present and functioning at their best. You will find that workgroup KM networks depend on the same critical components that information systems networks depend on:

- **Network:** A communication system that transmits information between nodes.

- **Hubs:** Centralized connecting devices that join communication lines together in a star configuration. Passive hubs are just connecting units that add nothing to the data passing through them; active hubs amplify the data bits in order to maintain a strong signal; and intelligent hubs provide added functionality.

- **Hosts:** Sources of information or signals. In network architectures, a client is also considered a host because it is a source of information to the network, in contrast to a router, which directs traffic.

- **Clients:** Standalone nodes on a network; can be both sources and/or destinations of information or signals. Usually, the client provides the goals.

- **Servers:** Nodes in a network that work for and are shared by multiple clients. Usually they possess the ability to perform functions at a high rate of efficiency.

- **Client/server:** In a client/server environment, the processing for the client is divided between one or more servers; often one server is used for application processing and another is used for database processing. This three-tier system is common in large enterprises.

- **Protocols:** Rules governing transmitting and receiving information. A set of rules that allow different resources to coordinate with each other without ambiguity.

- **Routers:** Forward information from one network to another. Based on routing tables and routing protocols, routers decide how to send information.

- **Bridges:** Connect two network segments together, which may be of similar or dissimilar types. Bridges learn from experience and build and maintain address tables of the network nodes. By monitoring which station acknowledged receipt of the address, they learn which nodes belong to the segment.

Networking issues among employees in a corporation are more complex than the hardware issues in information systems networking, but there are many similarities. The terminology and tactics of physical network troubleshooting do not always provide an effective framework for developing workgroup KM strategies, but they can provide a place to start.

In information systems, the general troubleshooting methodology is based on a three-step method of detection, isolation, and repair. Detect the problem, isolate it to a particular component, and then repair or replace the component. Social networks differ from technological networks in that they derive more strength from adaptation rather than optimization. They are similar in that they both try to balance the competing forces of diversity and compatibility to facilitate communication.

**Three Common Networking Problems**

❑ Your entire network is unreachable.

❑ You cannot connect to specific resources using their domain name server (DNS) names.

❑ You can connect to resources on the local subnet only.

TABLE 8.1 **Networking Diagnoses**

| Entire network unreachable | Have you selected the correct protocol? |
|---|---|
| | Networks rely on clearly defined, shared protocols. When, where, and how you say something makes all of the difference in whether you will be heard or ignored. |
| DNS names don't work | Is the DNS server down? |
| | In a network, a DNS server facilitates communication between resources that are linked through less formal methods than standard protocols call for. |
| Local subnet access only | Are you connected to a working router? |
| | There are likely to be several routers on your network. They prioritize and filter information flow across the network. Correcting your communication with the router opens doors. Use the wrong protocol with a key router and you will be very lonely. |

# Investing in Your Social Network

Detecting flaws in your social network should not be too much of a problem. A breakdown in your social network is as obvious as a breakdown in a computer network. Finding the cause of the breakdown is the next challenge, and if you plan on fixing the problem, you can expect to invest some social capital to do it.

> **Social capital: The ability to communicate with others, from both inside and outside of your organization, for information, advice, and solutions.**

Think of your social network as a database of "who knows what" and "who knows who." In other words, manage links to the knowledge rather than the knowledge itself. These links can be simply thought of as relationships. The currency of relationships is social capital. By demonstrating behaviors that value people and their needs, you increase your social capital and your chances of being successful.

## Four Types of Relationships

There are four types of relationships that you are certain to see in almost any environment: dependent, independent, counterdependent, and interdependent. These types of relationships appear in families, workgroups, churches, schools, and every other kind of social group. Notice that I said types of relationships, not types of people.

Relationships change over time. Yesterday we were dependent on our parents and today we are independent—sometimes the cycle goes full circle. These relationships are not set in stone; they are fluid. On some level, we choose to be interdependent or counterdependent based on how we perceive the situation.

Too often we have relationships that are counterdependent. In counterdependent relationships, each partner questions everything the other is doing, especially motives. This can often be seen in sibling relationships. Two children, partnered by nature as brother and sister, compete bitterly for their parents' affection. This unhealthy rivalry often leads to lifelong separation and mutual distrust. In a work environment, counterdependent relationships almost always lead to a lack of efficient information exchange—or worse.

> **Counterdependency: A behavioral defense in which people think of themselves as highly independent and self-sufficient. They find no value in anyone's efforts but their own.**

For example, in the oil industry, gasoline retailers sell gasoline and get a percentage of the margin between their costs and the market price of gas. Traditionally, oil companies try to reduce those margins to make them as low as possible. The oil suppliers believe that this is revenue they are losing. The resellers base their businesses on this margin, so they defend it with all of the resources they can muster. This highly adversarial situation causes the relationship between reseller and wholesaler to become counterdependent. Counterdependent relationships lead to minimal information exchange.

Because of lack of trust, participants in counterdependent relationships end up spending their time locked in combat, rather than pursuing the type of partnership on which their mutual success must be based. Resellers fail to provide consistent and accurate demand information to their suppliers, and suppliers fail to provide consistent and accurate supply information back to retailers. This vicious cycle limits the knowledge and agility of all players. It's a lose-lose situation that is far too common in business today.

On the workgroup level, counterdependent relationships are just as common and destructive as in the previous example. Consider a team that is tasked with choosing an enterprise recruiting software package. To make the process fair, the corporate office has populated the team with members from each major business unit. Each member is tasked with providing the team with detailed information on their recruiting system needs and voting for the choice that will best meet their goals.

Traditionally, all business groups in the enterprise compete in several areas. They compete for budget monies, headcount, floor space, and other resources. Years of competition have made these groups bitter and distrustful of one another. Each member brings a different agenda to the table. One group may be heavy recruiters and demand the highest level of functionality from their system. Another group may recruit so infrequently that their key demand is a low-cost system that minimizes the impact to their departmental budget; however, making the best enterprise software choice depends on finding a compromise solution. Success depends on building an environment of *interdependency.*

> **Interdependency: Mutual dependence. Behavior that recognizes that each of us needs and can benefit from working cooperatively with others.**

### Four Keys to Interdependent Relationships

1. *Security.* Protection from attack is perhaps the most basic of all group functions. In other words: "In the valley of the dinosaurs, all men are friends." Giving co-workers the idea that you want to ruin their careers destroys any hope of forming an interdependent relationship. Avoid adopting an I-win/you-lose orientation.

2. *Commonality.* A feeling of shared destiny and a recognition of the duty of each individual to contribute to and, if necessary, sacrifice for the group. People and organizations need each other. Organizations need ideas, energy, innovation, and talent; people need careers, salaries, peer recognition, and opportunities. We are all interdependent.

Consider using more permanent groups. Groups tend to develop through distinct phases, the first of which demands a great deal of attention to social concerns. As a result, continually forming new groups can lead to social awkwardness. Output from newly formed groups will not be as strong as if each collection of people were allowed to develop norms of comfort through repeated interaction over time.

3. *Trust.* Trust must be developed primarily on the individual level. A certain amount of mistrust among competing groups is to be expected, but it is hoped that the individuals involved can develop a level of trust that is sufficient to allow collaboration. The basis of distrust is simple fear—of attack, abandonment, or ridicule.

Sports and games that allow your group to team up against others can help build better relationships internally. Church, community service, and charity work can all be helpful in providing you with opportunities to build trust and invest more capital into your social network. Working together outside of work to achieve a goal builds a foundation of mutual trust that will often spread to the work environment as well.

4. *Flexibility of thought.* Only by focusing on problem solving, information gathering, and truth at the expense of ego, passions, and polarized viewpoints can we have the flexibility of thought that successful collaboration requires. Embrace a diversity of ideas and opinions when you encounter them. Combine advocacy (pursuing your own plan) with inquiry (listening to the other person) and test every assumption.

Workgroup interdependency is a worthy goal for any team, but it doesn't happen overnight. Newly developed teams will typically go through the same stages of development to arrive at interdependency that individuals go through. These stages are dependent, independent, and finally interdependent. You can set the stage for faster movement through these phases by demonstrating positive, people-valuing behavior, and the good news is that it makes work a much more fun place to be.

> *"There is a central difference between the old and new economies: the old industrial economy was driven by economies of scale; the new information economy is driven by the economics of networks."*
> —Carl Shapiro and Hal R. Varian, *Information Rules*

**Just for Fun**

Test how flexible your thinking is with this informal quiz:

**Example:** 16 = O in a P

**Answer:** 16 = ounces in a pound

| | | | |
|---|---|---|---|
| 1. | 26 = L of the A | 18. | 5 = D in Z C |
| 2. | 7 = D of the W | 19. | 57 = H V |
| 3. | 1001 = A N | 20. | 11 = P on a F T |
| 4. | 12 = S of the Z | 21. | 1000 = W that a P is W |
| 5. | 54 = C in a D | 22. | 29 = D in F in a L Y |
| 6. | 9 = P in the S S | 23. | 64 = S on a C B |
| 7. | 88 = PK | 24. | 40 = D and N of the G F |
| 8. | 13 = S on the A F | 25. | 76 = T in the B P |
| 9. | 32 = D F at which W F | 26. | 50 = W to L Y L |
| 10. | 18 = H on a G C | 27. | 99 = B of B on the W |
| 11. | 90 = D in a R A | 28. | 60 = S in a M |
| 12. | 200 = D for P G in M | 29. | 1 = H on a U |
| 13. | 8 = S on a S S | 30. | 9 = J on the S C |
| 14. | 3 = B M (S H T R) | 31. | 7 = B for S B |
| 15. | 4 = Q in a G | 32. | 21 = D on a D |
| 16. | 24 = H in a D | 33. | 7 = W of the A W |
| 17. | 1 = W on a U | 34. | 16 = M on a D M C |

**Scoring:**

1–6 Questions = Average

6–12 Questions = Somewhat intelligent

12–18 Questions = Intelligent

18+ Questions = Genius!

Answers at end of chapter.

# Phases of Team Development

Whether you are talking about sports teams or corporate implementation teams, researchers have determined that every developing team must go through certain stages. In 1965, Bruce Tuckman published a model for the life cycle of teams. It emphasized the following four key phases:

1. **Forming:** Players are brought together.
2. **Storming:** Players try to establish their place in the team.
3. **Norming:** Standards of behavior are set up.
4. **Performing:** Your players work together to win.

## Making the Team

When forming a team, consider the basic skills needed by members of the group. Four types of people are needed. They are:

- ❏ **Client:** This person has vision and creative problem-solving abilities.
- ❏ **Server:** This person knows how to get the job done on a technical level.
- ❏ **Hub:** This person is able to plan and organize how resources will be distributed.
- ❏ **Router:** This person can take an individual goal and transform it into a group goal.

When organizing a team, assemble in the group people who possess one or more of each of these four qualities. The input of each is critical in achieving a productive, well-balanced team. The best decisions come from teams in which everyone is committed to contributing and working together.

## Forming

Forming is an orientation period. The team members are not sure what their tasks are, they don't know what sort of a team leader they have, and they are not well acquainted with each other. Do not expect a great deal of trust and open communication at this point. Team members will tend to respond to the leader's requests and express few if any negative feelings.

During this first phase, the team leader needs to empower the members, reduce fear, and set guidelines for accomplishing tasks. One way to facilitate this is by soliciting team members' ideas, by asking open-ended questions and complimenting them when appropriate.

## Storming

In the storming phase, members should start feeling more comfortable together. Some may even challenge the team leader's authority and recommendations. Other members may challenge not only what the team is to do and how it is doing it, but also the leader's role and style of leadership.

> Do *not* try to avoid this somewhat more confrontational phase. A team that does not go through the storming phase will not develop adequate processes to deal with conflict.

This leads to teams that are passive, fragmented, and much less creative. In fact, some would say they are not teams at all. There needs to be a sorting-out period where each member can define his or her role.

### Norming

Norming further defines what was learned in the storming phase. Work out problems and strengthen group ties in this phase. Teams on larger projects should concentrate on establishing procedures for handling conflicts, decisions, and unexpected project issues. Focus on activities that empower team members, create trust, provide a vision of what the team can become, and teach decision-making and conflict management skills.

### Performing

Performing is the serious action phase. By now the team should have built some positive relationships, defined its tasks, and started to produce results. By learning how to work together, manage conflict, and share resources, the team has become interdependent, agile, and effective. It is a team that works!

### Additional Learning Resources

- ❑ *Information Rules: A Strategic Guide to the Network Economy*, by Carl Shapiro and Hal R. Varian (1998)
- ❑ *Social Network Analysis: Methods and Applications*, by Stanley Wasserman et al. (1994)
- ❑ *Linked: The New Science of Networks*, by Albert-László Barabási (2002)
- ❑ *The Secret Handshake: Mastering the Politics of the Business Inner Circle*, by Kathleen Kelly Reardon, Ph.D. (2000)
- ❑ *The Team-Building Workshop*, by Vivette Payne (2001)
- ❑ *Small Pieces Loosely Joined: A Unified Theory of the Web*, by David Weinberger (2002)
- ❑ http://www.hyperorg.com—*Journal of the Hyperlinked Organization*

## Answers to "Just for Fun" Exercise

1. 26 = L of the A—Letters of the Alphabet
2. 7 = D of the W—Days of the Week

3. 1001 = A N—Arabian Nights

4. 12 = S of the Z—Signs of the Zodiac

5. 54 = C in a D—Cards in a Deck

6. 9 = P in the S S—Planets in the Solar System

7. 88 = PK—Piano Keys

8. 13 = S on the A F—Stripes on the American Flag

9. 32 = D F at which W F—Degrees Fahrenheit at which Water Freezes

10. 18 = H on a G C—Holes on a Golf Course

11. 90 = D in a R A—Degrees in a Right Angle

12. 200 = D for P G in M—Dollars for Passing Go in Monopoly

13. 8 = S on a S S—Sides on a Stop Sign

14. 3 = B M (S H T R)—Blind Mice (See How They Run)

15. 4 = Q in a G—Quarts in a Gallon

16. 24 = H in a D—Hours in a Day

17. 1 = W on a U—Wheel on a Unicycle

18. 5 = D in Z C—Digits in a Zip Code

19. 57 = H V—Heinz Varieties

20. 11 = P on a F T—Players on a Football Team

21. 1000 = W that a P is W—Words that a Picture is Worth

22. 29 = D in F in a L Y—Days in February in a Leap Year

23. 64 = S on a C B—Squares on a Checker Board

24. 40 = D and N of the G F—Days and Nights of the Great Flood

25. 76 = T in the BP—Trombones in the Big Parade

26. 50 = W to L Y L—Ways to Leave Your Lover

27. 99 = B of B on the W—Bottles of Beers on the Wall

28. 60 = S in a M—Seconds in a Minute

29. 1 = H on a U—Horn on a Unicorn

30. 9 = J on the S C —Jurors on the Supreme Court

31. 7 = B for S B—Brides for Seven Brothers

32. 21 = D on a D—Dots on a Die

33. 7 = W of the A W—Wonders of the Ancient World

34. 16 = M on a D M C—Men on a Dead Man's Chest

**Test Your Knowledge**

## Discussion Questions

1.  What do you need to be able to capture knowledge?

2.  What affects knowledge flows in an organization?

3.  How do abstractions change how you perceive an idea?

4.  Where, in your opinion, does innovation happen?

5.  What would your definition of a workgroup be?

6.  What are the components of a workgroup?

7.  Do you have a social network?

## Review Questions

1. Our human ability to create _____ abstractions empowers us to understand complex systems.

2. Each of us use different abstractions based on our own unique _____ and _____.

3. This _____ of abstractions often causes communication problems, but it can be a source for new insights and innovations.

4. Knowledge flows _____ _____ in large, centralized, hierarchical organizations.

5. Because we all use different abstractions to understand the _____ that surround us, we all have different pictures of the situation.

6. Case studies of collaboration groups working within large corporations, such as Whirlpool, Eastman Kodak, and Hewlett-Packard, show that the _____ _____ of a team is typically based on an underlying network of social relationships.

7. The alignment of the various personal and business goals of these individuals is the difference between a painful _____ and a vibrant knowledge network.

8. Social networks differ from technologic networks in that they derive strength from _____ rather than optimization.

9. A breakdown in your social network is as _____ as a breakdown in a computer network.

10. By demonstrating behaviors that value people and their needs, you increase your _____ _____ and your chances of being successful.

11. In counterdependent relationships, each partner _____ everything the other is doing, especially motives.

12. Because of lack of _____, participants in counterdependent relationships end up spending their time locked in _____, rather than pursuing the type of partnership on which their mutual success must be based.

13. When _____ a team, consider the basic skills needed by members of the group.

14. Forming is an _____ period.

15. In the storming phase, members should start feeling more _____ together.

## Chapter Vocabulary

**Bureaucracy:** Management marked by hierarchical authority among numerous offices and by fixed procedures.

**Counterdependency:** A behavioral defense in which people think of themselves as highly independent and self-sufficient, finding value in only their own efforts.

**Diversity:** Displaying a multiplicity of difference and variety.

**Infrastructure:** The basic facilities, services, and installations needed for the functioning of a community or society.

**Intangibles:** Assets that cannot be easily perceived by the senses.

**Interdependency:** Mutually dependent behavior that recognizes that each of us needs and can benefit from working cooperatively with others.

**Metcalfe's Law:** Networking rule stating that the value of a network increases exponentially with the number of nodes; $Utility = (Nodes)^2$.

**Polarized:** Concentrated around two conflicting or contrasting positions.

**Social capital:** The ability to communicate with others, from both inside and outside of your organization, for information, advice, and solutions.

**Social network:** Your personal list of "who knows what" and "who knows who."

**Workgroup:** Any two or more individuals sharing information.

**Chapter**

**9**

# 3D Communication

*Secrecy is the enemy of trust and is responsible for much of the distrust that exists between business and society, corporations and customers, management and employees. . . . Openness allows all who are impacted to evaluate the decision. It creates a sense of integrity about the process—it promotes trust.*

—Keshavan Nair, *A Higher Standard of Leadership: Lessons from the Life of Gandhi*

*You can't not communicate. Everything you say and do or don't say and don't do sends a message to others.*

—John Woods

**Chapter Nine Learning Objectives**

- ❑ Understand the roles of timing and escalation in 3D communication.
- ❑ See why dialog is typically the most exciting method of communication and why it is not always the most suitable method for a given situation.
- ❑ Recognize the importance of common goals in forming teams.
- ❑ Learn that people's actions often work in the opposite direction of their expressed philosophy.
- ❑ Learn to utilize effective listening techniques.

How employees communicate internally is vital to the group's ability to resolve issues. Managers who continually communicate only by specifically directing others' actions are not able to reap the experience of their subordinates. In the business world, this is often referred to as **micromanaging**. Regardless of what they say, bosses are not all knowing and all seeing. They are going to miss a lot. In defense of managers, it must be said that highly technical workers often let their poor communication skills wreck their chances of success. Like families, the relationships between

---

technicians and management may often seem dysfunctional, but the fact is that they need each other desperately.

> **Micromanage: To direct or control in an overly detailed, often meddlesome manner.**

To improve communications, relationships, and the creation of knowledge products, we propose the 3D Communication Method: dialogue, discussion, and direction. Timing and escalation play a significant role in 3D communications and influence whether the communication process will be proactive or reactive. The manager's and subordinates' personalities can also make determining which communication method to use much more complicated.

The following table was designed to assist you in recognizing when to use dialogue, discussion, or direction in order to most effectively achieve your objectives. Team leaders often get caught up in using the wrong communication method for a given situation. This leads to frustration and intransigence on the part of team members, loss of confidence among stakeholders, and an overall lack of knowledge growth among all team members. Remember that none of these communication methods is inherently better or worse than the other methods; they are just different.

TABLE 9.1 **Recognizing the 3D Communication Methods**

| (1) Dialogue | (2) Discussion | (3) Direction |
|---|---|---|
| Proactive | Reactive | Reactive |
| No filtering except tact | Some filtering | Total filtering |
| Communicate openly | Communicate resources needs, timeframes, risks, assumptions, and limitations | Communicate individual responsibility, accountability measures, and vision of success |
| Few boundaries | Semistructured focus on the agenda | Strict focus on project timelines, resources, and objectives |
| Similar to brainstorming | Forming scope document and project plan | Executing project plan |
| Produces innovation, exposes assumptions, and broadens understanding | Produces schedules, plans, and processes | Produces actions, results, and responsibility |
| Working from diverse abstractions | Merges abstractions | Abstractions become decisions and tasks |

Successful team communication demands knowing when to enter into each of the three dimensions of 3D communication and when to move to the next level. Dialogue is typically the most fun and exciting dimension of communication, but it is not always the most suitable method for a given situation. Mountain climbing can provide a useful abstraction to look at the different dimensions of team communication.

# A Successful Ascent

Large-scale mountain expeditions require preparations that usually begin at least 12 months in advance of the climb. The time scales will vary according to the difficulty of the expedition (i.e., is it local, within the same country, visiting another country, in hazardous terrain, logistically difficult), but the following is a typical planning schedule:

**12–15 months before the ascent:**

Begin team building dialogues, fundraising and initial research, gain permissions, and produce a budget outline.

**8 months before the ascent:**

Schedule transportation and accommodation, arrange passports, visas, and letters of introduction, conduct physical training, etc.

Although the timeframe of your team's project may not be as large as climbing Mt. Everest, the phases are quite similar, and the need for proper communication throughout the mission is identical.

### Planning the Ascent = Dialogue Phase

Planning is essential to a successful expedition; in this stage surprises can be reduced to a manageable level without the safety of the team being compromised. Keys to success are starting early, questioning goals and assumptions, brainstorming contingencies, and tapping the combined experiences of the entire team. This should be a growth stage for everyone on the team, and success depends on a high degree of dialogue.

Many team members may express frustration and a strong ambition to begin the climb immediately. Real growth takes time; to gain commitment from the team, each member must participate fully in the dialogue. Work hard to address and resolve any reservations among team members at this point because they will be much more destructive at base camp.

### Preparation for the Ascent = Discussion Phase

A base camp's primary function is mission support in preparation of the ascent. Time is taken to safeguard and secure people, facilities, equipment, supplies, transportation networks, and information. Base camp functions must adapt to the current risks, mission, and objectives of its environment. This means base camp decisions are a function of resources, politics, and time and consequently require a greater degree of command and control than planning. There is less room for open-ended dialogue because of the somewhat dangerous conditions (e.g., weather, altitude, nerves, competition) of base camp, yet the unpredictability of the situation calls for more dialogue than at the final stage. Discussions at this point must remain focused on the objective.

Growth of individual team members is still in progress at base camp (acclimatizing, training, situational analysis), although at a slower rate than during the planning phase. Expect to meet with naysayers, prophets of doom, and other experienced experts who will assure you that success is not possible. This will test the team's resolve. Unfortunately, by the time you reach base camp, the amount of resources invested makes changing the objective practically impossible.

Key activities conducted at base camp include the following:
- Discussing environmental conditions
- Finalizing roles and responsibilities
- Debating individual approaches to the summit
- Approving packing lists
- Assessing weather conditions
- Scheduling the tasks required for the ascent

### Making the Ascent = Direction Phase

An entire year of planning has gone into the ascent. Often, weeks must be spent at base camp waiting for the proper conditions. The ascent must be completed in five hours because being on the summit at nightfall means almost certain death. During the ascent, there can be no question of who is the team's leader. The stakes are now high, and the need for coordinated action is absolute. Open dialogue at this point is worse than useless; it is dangerous to the entire team and the objective.

Communication can and must occur throughout the mission, but care must be taken to have the appropriate type of discussions. Strictly controlled, agenda-focused discussions during the planning (dialogue) phase are sure to gloss over differences of opinion and fail to bring critical assumptions to light. Lengthy, open-ended, dialogues during the preparation (discussion) phase endangers the timeline and risks losing team cohesiveness.

In the implementation (direction) phase, the team must operate as a single, cohesive unit in order to successfully attack the target. That requires firm leadership and a much stronger adherence to the chain of command. It might seem counterintuitive, but it takes real courage to delegate. To give a subordinate the authority to perform a function and then to stand aside and let him or her risk possible failure takes valor. Don't assume that complaints and arguments at this stage are harmless—they are not!

It is no coincidence that countless ancient cultures have chosen mountains as sacred spaces and have considered the ascent of those peaks as the task of heroes and holy men. Accomplishing large tasks requires confidence, commitment, inner strength, and clarity of purpose, but the most important thing it requires is a team that can collaborate effectively.

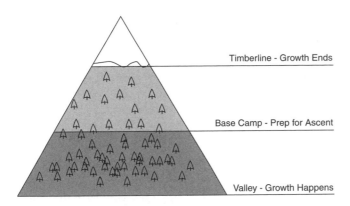

Timberline - Growth Ends

Base Camp - Prep for Ascent

Valley - Growth Happens

FIGURE 9.1 **The Mountain.**

# Building Teams That Work

*To effectively communicate, we must realize that we are all different in the way we perceive the world and use this understanding as a guide to our communication with others.*

—Anthony Robbins

Teams are groups of people working together toward common goals. Without a common goal, there is no team. Team members should come from all walks of life, in order to provide unique backgrounds and perspectives. These differences bring diversity to the team, which is an important factor in team performance.

Teams have many advantages over individuals working in isolation. Teams are normally better at solving problems, have a higher level of commitment, and include more people who can help implement an idea or plan. Moreover, teams are able to generate energy and interest in new projects.

For a team to be at its best, individual team members need to have a sense of commitment, shared goals, the ability to work together, mutual accountability, and access to any needed resources and skills.

### Mutual Accountability: How to Get There

As a project manager, you typically walk into the project kickoff meeting with a distinct advantage over the other team members. You have been told what tasks you have to complete to be personally successful. If you have accepted the philosophy presented in this book, you will have the goal of maximizing the dissemination and discussion of valid information. You will also want to avoid the conflict that results from knowledge hoarding. This means that your fellow team members will also need to know what they will have to achieve to be personally successful. This requires communication; how you communicate has a huge bearing on your ability to be successful.

Walk into your meetings ready to present to each team member a list of the tasks/deliverables they need to handle in order to be personally successful. Too many project managers avoid doing this and instead prefer to place their own objective as the personal objective of each team member. For project managers, personal success means project completion as originally planned before the first kickoff meeting. Often, they have already selected and filtered the relevant data (leaving only the data that supports the idea they are advocating), set the timeframe for delivery, and determined what the costs will be.

This leaves the team with the task of delivering what they never promised, promoted, or even advocated. It robs the team of the opportunity to frame the issues, collect information, and create a reasonable project schedule. Project managers who work this way are stuck in an obsolete mode of corporate thinking.

## A New Model of Thinking

Chris Argyris and Donald Schön, pioneering Action Science experts, express this as Model I thinking, which utilizes the following strategies:

### Strategies of Model I
- ❑ Define goals and try to achieve them through power games.
- ❑ Maximize personal wins and minimize personal losses.
- ❑ Minimize expressing negative feelings or observations.
- ❑ Display rationality and minimize showing emotions.

Overall, it doesn't sound that bad, does it? In practice, this line of thinking leads to the following team tactics:

### Fundamental Operating Logic of Model I
- ❑ Design, manage, and plan unilaterally.
- ❑ Own and control the high-level task.
- ❑ Hoard valid information.
- ❑ Unilaterally protect self and allies.
- ❑ Evaluate others in ways that will not be tested for validity.
- ❑ Recognize only your personal victories.

This mode of thinking leads to the classic corporate work environment of endless tribal warfare. If you follow this outdated philosophy, you will almost certainly see all or some of the following consequences:

### Consequences of Model I Thinking
- ❑ Defensiveness
- ❑ Mistrust
- ❑ Unhealthy competition

- ❏ Interpersonal manipulation
- ❏ Rapid employee burnout rate
- ❏ Tribalism
- ❏ Conformity in thinking
- ❏ Power games
- ❏ Low freedom of choice
- ❏ Low internal commitment
- ❏ Low risk taking
- ❏ Ineffective learning
- ❏ Little rigorous testing of assumptions
- ❏ Decreased effectiveness
- ❏ A focus on details of marginal relevance
- ❏ An inability to address fundamental problems

Argyris and Schön promote the following new model of thinking in order to facilitate collaborative team learning and organizational effectiveness. It is interesting to note that while Model I thinking is most often observed in a corporate environment, most of the Model I thinkers will *express* a belief in Model II thinking that is not reflected in their actions. Argyris and Schön refer to this as a disconnection between espoused theories and theories in use.

### Fundamental Features of Model II Thinking

- ❏ Seek out disconfirming evidence.
- ❏ Balance advocacy and inquiry.
- ❏ Test out facts and assumptions.
- ❏ Utilize reflective thinking and dialogue to root out inconsistencies.
- ❏ Use multiple independent information sources.
- ❏ Encourage the expression of diverse opinions—even (gasp!) controversy.
- ❏ Share all valid information, but share it tactfully.
- ❏ Seek out win-win solutions.
- ❏ Build flatter hierarchies, so that team members can originate ideas and actions.

The thinking model proposed can often feel more like a moral/ethical model than a thought process. Ideas such as tact, tolerance, openness, and fairness may seem more familiar in the realm of social services than the dog-eat-dog world of corporate America, but these ideas go to the heart of what makes human relationships tick.

> *"Being listened to is so close to being loved that most people cannot tell the difference."*
> —David Oxberg

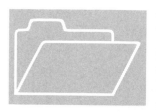

### Case Study: Saturn Corp.'s Web Presence

The automobile maker Saturn Corp. has more than 370 independent retailers. Potential customers visit the Saturn Website and ask about certain cars. Saturn takes these contacts seriously. First, they automatically send all requests to the appropriate dealers, so that the dealers can follow-up on their leads the following business day. By immediately generating confirmation receipts, customers are informed of the status of their requests and that their feedback is valued. The car you choose and the options you add are all right in front of the salesperson when he or she contacts you later. Finally, to ensure quality, the Saturn Web team contacts each retailer that received a lead and verifies that the customer was dealt with promptly.

These days, all of the Saturn retailers are promptly following up on Internet leads, because they now get more than 70% of their new customer prospects from their Website. Saturn quickly realized that a Website is much more than mere advertising. A Website provides an *interface* to your customers, and that is as vital to your business as the smile on your face. Companies that develop clear, efficient processes for listening to what their customers are interested in make it easy to do business with them, as well as increasing revenues, decreasing transaction costs, and building customer loyalty. The key is to do both follow-up and follow-through on *all* contacts.

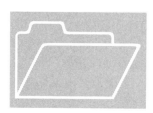

### Case Study: From Candles to Soap

In late 1879, Procter and Gamble's main business was producing and selling candles; however, Thomas Edison's invention of the light bulb looked as if it would make candles completely obsolete. In just a few years, the market for candles had plummeted to all-time lows. Things looked bad for P&G at this time, and it seemed that the company's destiny might lie in bankruptcy court, but the fate of a company lies in the minds and hearts of its employees.

One day a forgetful P&G worker at a small factory in Cincinnati forgot to turn off his machine when he went to lunch. The result of this carelessness was that air bubbles worked their way into a huge batch of soap mixture, making it a frothy mess! After discussing it with his supervisor, they decided not to discard the soap mixture. The soap hardened and then it was cut, packaged, and shipped to customers as if nothing went wrong.

About a month later, P&G received orders for more of "the floating soap." The sales department was perplexed, but some detective work finally solved the mystery. The air bubbles mixed into the soap had made it lighter than water, so it floated. The process also made each bar of Ivory smoother and easier to lather. The workman's error eventually became the mainstay of P&G. You see, at that time, many people bathed in rivers and creeks. Floating soap would never sink and so it was rarely lost. Ivory soap consequently became a best-seller across the country, and P&G learned how a crisis could become an opportunity—by listening!

Business leaders consistently rank listening as one the top five skills they look for in employees. Effective listening techniques empowers those who utilize it. Although speaking is often held up as the way to influence people, good listeners can also have a powerful effect on those around them. Speakers share knowledge and attempt to persuade, but listeners make the decisions on what information to act on. The audience always determines whether a speaker was successful, which is why we say that **listening gives you power**.

### Dialogue

This is a moral/ethical dilemma that was once actually used as part of a job application.

You are driving along in your car on a wild, stormy night. You pass by a bus stop, and you see three people waiting for the bus:

1. An old lady who looks as if she is about to die

2. An old friend who once saved your life

3. The perfect man (or) woman you have been dreaming about

Which one would you choose to offer a ride to, knowing that there could only be one passenger in your car?

You could pick up the old lady because she is going to die, and thus you should save her first; or you could take the old friend because he or she once saved your life, and this would be the perfect chance to pay him or her back; however, you may never be able to find your perfect dream lover again.

The candidate who was hired (out of 200 applicants) had no trouble coming up with his answer. (I love this. You may actually use it some time for an interview situation.)

### What Did He Say?

He simply answered: "I would give the car keys to my old friend, and let him take the old lady to the hospital. I would stay behind and wait for the bus with the woman of my dreams."

Many times a little creative thinking can change a win-lose scenario into a win-win scenario.

### Additional Learning Resources

❑ *Theory in Practice: Increasing Professional Effectiveness*, by Chris Argyris and Donald A. Schon (1992)

❑ *The Five Dysfunctions of a Team: A Leadership Fable*, by Patrick M. Lencioni (2002)

❑ *The Right Mountain: Lessons from Everest on the Real Meaning of Success*, by Jim Hayhurst (1997)

❑ *How the Way We Talk Can Change the Way We Work: Seven Languages for Transformation*, by Robert Kegan and Lisa Laskow Lahey (2000)

## Test Your Knowledge

### Discussion Questions

1. What is important in communicating with others?

2. Do you always communicate in the same way?

3. What changes your communication patterns?

4. Is it important to plan to communicate? Why?

5. How does planned communication differ from spontaneous communication?

6. Is it okay to disagree when communicating?

7. How do you grow through communication?

8. Does communication bring accountability? Why?

### Review Questions

1. _____ is the enemy of trust and is responsible for much of the distrust that exists between business and society, corporations and customers, management and employees.

2. Managers who continually communicate only by specifically _____ their actions are not able to reap the experience of their subordinates.

3. Timing and _____ play a significant role in 3D communications and influence whether the communication process will be proactive or reactive.

4. Dialogue is typically the most _____ and _____ dimension of communication, but it is not always the most suitable method for a given situation.

5. _____ is essential to a successful expedition; in this stage surprises can be reduced to a manageable level without the safety of the team being affected.

6. Real growth takes time; to gain commitment from the team, each member must participate fully in the _____.

7. Growth of individual team members is still in progress at base camp (acclimatizing, training, situational analysis), although at a slower rate than during the _____ phase.

8. Strictly controlled, _____-focused discussions during the planning phase are sure to gloss over differences of opinion and fail to bring critical assumptions to light.

9. Accomplishing large tasks requires confidence, commitment, inner strength, and clarity of purpose, but the most important thing it requires is a team that can _____ effectively.

10. Without a common _____, there is no team.

11. Ideas such as tact, tolerance, openness, and fairness may seem more familiar in the realm of _____ _____ than the dog-eat-dog world of corporate America, but these ideas go to the heart of what makes human relationships tick.

## Chapter Vocabulary

**3D communication:** Communication method based on the timely usage of dialogue, discussion, and direction to achieve business objectives and maximize the learning and growth of team members.

**Accountability:** Liable to being called to account; answerable.

**Dialogue:** An exchange of ideas or opinions among two or more people.

**Direction:** The act of directing, aiming, regulating, guiding, or ordering an action or operation.

**Discussion:** A formal, structured discourse on a topic.

**Dissemination:** To spread abroad or scatter widely.

**Escalation:** An increase to counteract a perceived discrepancy.

**Filtering:** Removing unwanted elements by passing through a filter, as in filtering out impurities.

**Hierarchies:** Groups ordered into separate ranks each subordinate to the one above it.

**Micromanage:** To direct or control in an overly detailed, often meddlesome manner.

**Objective:** Something worked toward or striven for. Also can mean uninfluenced by emotions or personal prejudices.

**Proactive:** Acting in advance to deal with an expected difficulty.

**Reactive:** Tending to be responsive or to react to a stimulus.

**Tact:** Acute sensitivity to what is proper and appropriate in dealing with others, including the ability to speak or act without offending.

**Unilateral:** Of, on, relating to, involving, or affecting only one side.

# Building in Knowledge Exchange

*A powerful global conversation has begun. Through the Internet, people are discovering and inventing new ways to share relevant knowledge with blinding speed. As a direct result, markets are getting smarter—and getting smarter faster than most companies.*

—Rick Levine, Christopher Locke, Doc Searls, and David Weinberger,
*The Cluetrain Manifesto*

### Chapter Ten Learning Objectives

- ❑ Realize that you cannot avoid knowledge exchange, but you can limit or improve your opportunities for mutual learning.
- ❑ See every social relationship as a potential channel for years of knowledge exchange and mutual learning.
- ❑ Know that good leadership calls for balancing advocacy with inquiry.
- ❑ Understand that successful collaborative learning requires access to information, attention, and engagement from all parties involved.

I n the last chapter, we introduced a model of thinking that was designed to improve the learning that occurs among team members attempting to collaborate effectively. There is something to be learned from every relationship, and a KM strategy seeks to maximize that learning for all parties involved. When looking for new learning opportunities, don't overlook your best resources—your customers, suppliers, and co-workers.

Every communication represents a knowledge exchange. You cannot avoid this exchange, but you can limit or improve the opportunities for mutual learning. Attempts at secrecy will typically only result in mistrust, misjudgments, and false information. The best strategy is to share knowledge with the goal of maximizing mutual learning. Naturally, this is easier said than done.

Product implementations, construction, procedural changes, new service offerings, and systems development all offer powerful opportunities to increase the potential for knowledge exchange within your business. Recognizing the potential knowledge exchange opportunities early in development will improve your chances of success.

To maximize mutual learning in your information exchange, begin looking for dialogue forums and more structured information flows. Consider what information the other party wants and/or needs early in your planning processes. In a recent survey of corporate librarians, the top five most common requests were:

1. Contact information for a co-worker (79%)

2. Company news (76%)

3. Press coverage mentioning the company (60%)

4. Press coverage about another topic (52%)

5. Company policies (45%)

The irony of these statistics is that they represent information that is fairly easy to integrate into almost any new IT project. Most organizations have global address books of internal contact information that could provide pointers to specialists in a wide range of fields, if sufficient effort were put into updating them and integrating them with other systems. Unfortunately, the opportunity is too often squandered. Managing contact information is of such vital importance to any business that you ignore it at your own peril. Every social relationship is a potential channel for years of knowledge exchange and mutual learning.

# Channels for Knowledge Exchange

For the purpose of discussion, we have put together the following KM Channel Analysis Matrix to help analyze products and services for injecting knowledge exchange opportunities into them. This matrix is a good example of information tools that you should be building and adding to your intellectual toolkit.

| Matrix for Analyzing the Collection and Distribution of a Parking Meter Information | | | | | | | | |
|---|---|---|---|---|---|---|---|---|
| What Information is the Product Capable of Collecting? | Is the Information Being Captured? | Currently Receiving Information? | | | Interest Level Estimate | | | |
| | | Vendor | Implementer | Customers | Vendor | Implementer | Customers | Others |
| Meter location popularity | Yes | No | Yes | No | No | Yes | Yes | City Police |
| Avg. time per user | No | No | No | No | Maybe | Yes | Yes | Lot Owners |
| Age of hardware | Yes | No | Yes | No | Yes | Yes | Maybe | Municipalities |
| # of meters on block | Yes | No | Yes | No | Maybe | Yes | Yes | Chamber of Commerce |
| Is the meter currently available? | No | No | No | No | Maybe | Yes | Yes | City Planners |
| Credit card information | No | No | No | No | Maybe | Yes | Yes | Travel Agents |
| Cell phone information | No | No | No | No | Maybe | Yes | Yes | Towing Companies & Taxi Services |
| | | | | | | | | |
| | | | | | | | | |
| | | | | | | | | |
| | | | | | | | | |

FIGURE 10.1 **KM Channel Analysis Matrix.**

The matrix is broken down into four sections, to inspire creative thinking when trying to improve products. The first section is used to brainstorm "What information is the product capable of collecting?" The idea for this section is to try and think of as many different examples of information that the product could possibly collect. The first example is a parking meter. What information could the parking meter be made to collect?

The second section is used to document whether the information is currently being collected. It is important to know whether the information is already being collected because the product may be doing its part, but the analysis is breaking down somewhere else.

The third section breaks down who is receiving the information. This section is divided into three groups: vendors, implementers, and customers. These three groups will be used to describe the producer of the product (vendor), the middle group that implements the product for service use (implementer), and the final purchaser of the product (customer).

The fourth section shows the possibility of interest in the information by grouping. Today a group may be receiving the information but fail to see the value of it. The value of information is often lost in corporations. The focus tends to be in finding and eliminating the information that may harm the company and not in looking for the information that could produce a new product or service.

Join in this exercise to increase your understanding of this analysis process. Follow along as we describe this simple matrix to enhance brainstorming new knowledge exchange opportunities. The first product to analyze is the parking meter. Approach this analysis from an independent view. You do not represent the vendor, implementer, or customer. Your purpose is to simply improve the parking meter for the good of all humanity.

The first place to begin is with the information capture part of the operation. Consider what information is collected today, could be collected today, or could be collected today with changes to the parking meter. Every process has an information capture component. Some are just very poor. Record the results of your information capture brainstorming in the first section.

For this example, we have listed several ideas for information in the first column that we brainstormed for parking meters. The following columns are not too difficult to fill in and sometimes generate extra ideas. Have some fun with the matrix and see what you are able to come up with. Capture all ideas first, and then edit out the bad ideas later. At this stage, there are no bad ideas.

As stated previously, the KM Channel Analysis Matrix is a knowledge and information tool that we generated to enhance idea exchange within a group. It is important when building an analysis tool or improving one that the individuals who are participating in the design are sharing similar abstractions. A lot of strong discussion went into the creation of the template that is used, and during the early discussions we worked from different abstractions. Dialogue is the key to finding common ground between dissimilar abstractions.

**Case Study: The Sad Tale of the Vasa**

The year was 1628, the king, Gustavus Adolphus II, desired to make Sweden a naval superpower. He ordered a new warship, the Vasa, to be built that would rival all previous warships in size and technology. Before completing the design phase of the project, the king ordered that the keel be laid. Before the workmen were finished laying the Vasa's keel, the king ordered the ship to be made longer.

FIGURE 10.2 **King Gustavus Adolphus II.**

The master shipwright who was assigned to the project feared the hot-tempered king, so the change went unchallenged. The shipwright then took ill and had to direct the project from his sickbed and later died before the Vasa was completed. The king assigned the remainder of the project to the master shipwright's assistant. The project may still have been partially successful except for a final change that was ordered by the clueless king: a second gun deck.

The result of this tremendous effort was the most elaborate, technically advanced, and heaviest armed warship of its day, but one too long and too tall for its beam and ballast. The project had focused on features instead of the stability of the platform. After an unsuccessful stability test (the crew rocked the vessel by running from the port side to the starboard side), all other tests were canceled and the ship was readied for her maiden voyage.

FIGURE 10.3 **The Sinking of the Vasa.**

None of King Gustavus's officers or officials communicated the test failure to the king because he was impatiently waiting for the ship to be deployed to help in his war with Poland. Instead the ship set sail and attempted to put to sea. Minutes later, with all of her home port of Stockholm watching, the Vasa rolled over and sank, killing many of her crew. Far too often technically adept employees are overridden by politically savvy consultants and project managers who push the technical employees into their personal agendas. Had the good king listened *reflectively* to his builders and given them the confidence and trust to speak their minds, a terrible tragedy could have been avoided.

## Change Management

Individuals in businesses today often ignore or suppress valuable information; this makes change management a constant challenge. The complexity of managing change in diverse, globally distributed companies demands a greater focus on this issue. The rise of outsourcing emphasizes the need for better change management processes even more. The problem is often compounded by the differences in change management abstractions. Command-and-control-focused managers often use change management systems to support the status quo. Technical workers too often view the change management systems as worthless, time consumers, and needless bureaucracy. Change management systems should ensure open and widespread communications to reduce assumptions, duplication of effort, and missteps. The goal of change management systems is to disseminate knowledge of the details and implications of upcoming change—not to prop up the status quo.

In Chapter 1, we introduced the project scope triangle. Management of any project requires balancing the competing interests of cost, time, and functionality. When the king increased the cost and scope of functionality for the Vasa, without increasing the timeframe for completion, the triangle was broken. Good leadership calls for balancing advocacy with inquiry. *Remember:* Listen reflectively and test your assumptions.

FIGURE 10.4 **Scope Triangle.**

Change management runs into problems because people tend to focus on achieving the goals that they are advocating instead of balancing advocacy with inquiry. Inquiry not only helps confirm your assumptions, but also builds an environment of mutual learning. Using inquiry techniques such as reflective listening communicates to others that you are interested in their input and that you value it enough to put it to use. People rarely enjoy giving information if they think that the person receiving the information does not value it.

## Unexamined Assumptions Lead to Missed Opportunities

The typical department store credit card captures a wealth of data about every transaction. More and more consumers are beginning to wonder fearfully what is being done with this information. And why shouldn't they?

From my casual observation, I can tell you a few things my local merchants are not doing with my credit card information:

❑ Assisting me with remembering clothing size information for my wife and child

❑ Reminding me of anniversaries and birthdays

❑ Notifying me when items I regularly purchase are on sale

❑ Noticing how far I drive to visit their store and providing appropriate service

❑ Using their knowledge of me to help build a relationship between us

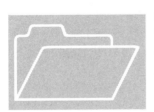

### Case Study: Documents That Improve Cross-Selling

The popular Applebee's restaurant chain has adopted a novel way to improve their service by building a new opportunity for knowledge exchange into their product. Although many restaurants in their class present customer bills in fancy leatherette or calfskin folders, Applebee's considers this last guest contact as a prime advertising (read: information exchange) opportunity.

The traditional embossing of "Thank You" on a check presenter provides little value to the customer and serves as a poor substitute for a real thank you. Applebee's uses small, beautifully illustrated versions of their dessert menus as check presenters. This offers an upselling/cross-selling opportunity to the server presenting the check, as well as an opportunity for the guest to ask any questions they may have about the desserts offered.

> **Attempting to sell add-ons or accessories with your products and services is a sales technique known as *cross-selling*. Promoting a higher level of product or service is called *upselling*.**

Both upselling and cross-selling are valuable services; they allow customers to fill their needs all at one time, rather than thinking of those needs and having to search for them later. These are not cheap sales tricks; they are powerful KM techniques that require actively listening to the customer's needs (voiced or not!), picking up on the clues, and then making recommendations based on experience and knowledge.

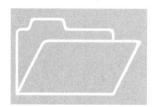

### Case Study: Documents That Improve Upselling

Okmulgee Plumbing provides local services in a field not usually known for valuing knowledge exchange. Instead of participating in the traditional "race to the bottom" strategy of strict competition based on price, Okmulgee Plumbing looks at its business as that of a localized service provider. Instead of merely fixing plumbing problems and installing new equipment, they make a firm effort to capture and maintain the *history* of every property they serve.

Because of the size of the business, the computer system needs for this endeavor are not huge; however, the payback for Okmulgee Plumbing is significant. By referring to the site histories they have collected, they are able to avoid merely repairing symptomatic problems and focus on fundamental solutions. These fundamental solutions are often higher-level products and services that improve their bottom line, as well as improving the reputation of their service personnel and the loyalty the customers have to Okmulgee Plumbing. This reputation of thoroughness has allowed them to command a higher price for their work in addition to increased repeat business.

Put a great deal of thought into every document you send out to your market. This means more than just having your lawyers sterilize every press release and quarterly report. Consider receipts, surveys, sales circulars, and so on as information delivery vehicles to increase the opportunities for knowledge exchange. Raise the understanding of your customers, and they will begin to value every communication you send them in a new way. Just as in other human relationships, openness leads to trust and creates the foundation of a functional relationship.

Don't just pay lip service to customer complaints. Customers who contact you with either praise or complaints are your best resource for improving your business. There is an old adage that says "Silence is golden." This old saying is accurate, if you take into consideration the difference between *gold* and *golden*. Golden typically means having a yellow color suggestive of gold. Gold is a metallic element, constituting the most precious metal used as a common commercial medium of exchange.

> **Silence is indeed golden, but conversations are gold!**

## The Return of Conversation

The quotation at the beginning of this chapter is from *The Cluetrain Manifesto*. This provocative and groundbreaking book introduces the idea of markets as conversations. A conversation represents exchanging thoughts, opinions, and feelings. In the past, marketplaces were a major center for conversations. Vendors and customers communicated face-to-face, and powerful partnerships were formed. Languages and cultures commingled and evolved in the chaotic and wonderful cornucopia of the marketplace.

Marketplaces were both civic attractions and nerve centers to gauge the pulse of the cities that contained them. The famous library at Alexandria, Egypt, was often considered the major learning center of the ancient world, but the real center of learning for most people was the local marketplace. It is no accident that great libraries like those at Alexandria were rare, but every city had a marketplace. In fact, you did not have a city without first having a marketplace.

Sadly, these dynamic marketplaces eventually became more rare as the philosophy of mass marketing grew in scope and capability. Conversations were whittled down to sterile press releases and focus groups. Businesses lost touch with their customers. True knowledge exchange was filtered and standardized away—sacrificed on the altar of mass communication and media. Although these tools have provided many benefits to modern business, these benefits have come at a price.

**Distinctions between mass media and conversations:**

| Conversations | Mass Media |
|---|---|
| Personalized service | Crafted broadcasts |
| Instant feedback | Delayed feedback |
| Difficult to scale | Highly scalable |
| Dialogues | Monologues |
| Largely analog | Largely digital |
| Build trust and community | Build brand awareness and recognition |
| Diversity | Conformity |
| People focused | Procedure focused |

### New Tools Clear Away Old Obstacles

Thankfully, the change appears to be coming full circle. Wave after wave of new communication technologies have taken the world by storm. E-mail, chat rooms, instant messaging, newsgroups, and the Web have created countless new forums for dialogue. It is also interesting to note that the collaboration tools mentioned previously were not the creation of massive communication companies. True innovation most often comes from small teams and individuals.

Collaboration tools empower companies and their customers to engage in discussions that would have been thought to be impossible just a few short years ago. One of the biggest challenges for today's companies is in deciding how to deploy these new technologies to effectively improve business performance. This is important because many companies have spent huge sums of money implementing technologies that are rarely, if ever, utilized. Successful collaborative learning requires access to information, attention, and engagement from all parties involved. *Remember:* Attention is the currency of the Information Age, and trust is the bandwidth.

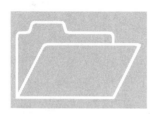

### Case Study: Dell Computer

Dell Computer Corporation provides an example of how conversations can be used to create competitive advantages. Central to Dell's strategy for creating value is its direct sales model, which offers in-person relationships with corporate and institutional customers; telephone and Internet purchasing; phone and online technical support; and next-day, on-site product service. Using Web technologies has allowed Dell to maintain an ongoing conversation among themselves, their customers, and their vendors.

This approach that Dell pioneered keeps them turning out products only when there is real demand. The result: Dell has developed a significant competitive advantage over the make-and-sell strategies of their competitors. By precisely sensing the types and kinds of product attributes that are important to various segments of its customer base, Dell forges strong direct and personal relationships with its customers. This allows them to be able to design better products and enables rapid response to customer demand while simultaneously reducing operating risks and costs. This strategy of valuing conversations with customers has helped to make Dell the world's leading direct computer systems sales company.

## Maximize Your Knowledge Exchange

Knowledge exchange is too difficult, costly, and time consuming to waste. Maximizing your knowledge exchange requires that you carefully examine all of your points of information exchange and search for improvements. Although it sounds simple, this goal can be extremely difficult to achieve.

It is especially difficult for large, highly structured corporations because successful knowledge exchange requires connectedness. After spending the last several decades developing cultures based on competition, compartmentalizing, and enforcing unilateral control, the current old guard is far from well prepared to move to a model of communication, collaboration, and constant learning. The following list contains a few strategies to implement into your project planning to get you started.

❑ Increase cooperation between businesspeople and technical specialists. Multi-disciplinary teams, job rotation programs, and "lunch and learn" programs provide new forums for developing better partnerships between these two groups.

❑ Look for managers with business experience and IT knowledge as well as strong general management skills.

❑ Increase the amount of automatic knowledge sharing by building collaboration into new systems. Work request management systems, help desk software, and ERP systems can typically be set up to allow you to share information between business groups with much less trouble.

❑ Watch for self-organizing groups to form and then work to keep them alive. A common example of a self-organizing group is a community whose members work together during a crisis. People in a crisis will often organize themselves based on their abilities, without using significant hierarchical structures. If employees take the time to explore their common interests and experiences before beginning work on a project, they are more likely to establish a camaraderie that will help them share information in the future.

❑ Look for ways to encourage project teams to spend time together in non–project-related environments. This builds the social capital of the team, while allowing each individual a glimpse into the abstractions of teammates.

Encouraging people to exchange knowledge freely is almost always a difficult proposition. Employees rarely want to cross-train anyone else to do their jobs. Yet, this is a critical function for the sustainability of the company. Sharing knowledge is too often seen as a threat to employee job security. Just knowing what information would be valuable if shared can be challenging.

New ways of leading, working, and thinking must be practiced until they become habitual. This change is not going to occur all at once across your company. Create small groups that foster trust, accountability, and openness. Spreading these ethics throughout your organization will be a long journey. Determining where to begin first in creating these environments is a subject that has become increasingly controversial over the last few years. Providing you with some suggestions of where to begin driving KM into your organizational structure will be the subject of Chapter 11.

## Additional Learning Resources

❑ *The Book of Management Wisdom: Classic Writings by Great Business Leaders*, edited by Peter Krass (1997)

❑ *Peopleware: Productive Projects and Teams*, 2nd ed., by Tom Demarco and Timothy R. Lister (1999)

❑ *Death March: The Complete Software Developer's Guide to Surviving "Mission Impossible" Projects*, by Edward Yourdon (1999)

❑ *The Cluetrain Manifesto: The End of Business as Usual,* by Christopher Locke, Rick Levine, Doc Searls, and David Weinberger (2001)

## Test Your Knowledge

## Discussion Questions

1. When looking at new learning opportunities, what should you consider?

2. When considering the survey of corporate librarians, what in your opinion is the availability of the requested information?

3. What could be improved on the KM Channel Analysis Matrix (see Figure 10.1)?

4. In your opinion, what was the most tragic part of the Vasa story? Why?

5. How could the Vasa tragedy have been avoided?

6. Because of the disaster of the Vasa, what has been learned? Can we learn from our disasters?

7. Give an example of upselling and cross-selling.

## Review Questions

1. There is something to be learned from every _____, and a KM strategy seeks to maximize that learning for all parties involved.

2. Every _____ represents a knowledge exchange.

3. Attempts at _____ will typically only result in mistrust, misjudgments, and false information.

4. To maximize mutual learning in your information exchange, begin looking for _____ _____ and more structured information flows.

5. Businesses today often ignore or suppress valuable _____; this makes change management a constant challenge.

6. _____ _____ runs into problems because people tend to focus on achieving the goals that they are advocating instead of balancing advocacy with inquiry.

7. Both _____ and _____ are valuable services; they allow the customer to fill their needs all at one time, rather than thinking of those needs and having to search for them later.

8. Put a great deal of _____ into every document you send out to your market.

9. Consider receipts, surveys, sales circulars, and so on as knowledge _____ _____.

10. Customers who _____ are one of your best resources for improving your business.

11. Silence is indeed _____, but conversations are gold.

12. A conversation represents _____ thoughts, opinions, and feelings.

13. Marketplaces were both civic attractions and _____ _____ to gauge the pulse of the cities that contained them.

14. Sadly, these _____ marketplaces eventually became more rare as the philosophy of mass marketing grew in scope and capability.

15. True knowledge exchange was filtered and _____ away, sacrificed on the alter of mass communication and media.

16. E-mail, chat rooms, instant messaging, newsgroups, and the Web have created countless new _____ for dialogue.

17. Collaboration tools empower companies and their customers to engage in _____ that would have been thought to be impossible just a few short years ago.

18. Knowledge _____ is too difficult, costly, and time consuming to waste.

19. After spending the last several decades developing cultures based on competition, compartmentalizing, and enforcing unilateral control, the current _____ _____ is far from well prepared to move to a model of communication, collaboration, and constant learning.

20. Employees rarely want to _____-_____ anyone else to do their jobs.

21. New ways of leading, working, and thinking must be practiced until they become _____.

## Chapter Vocabulary

**Brainstorming:** A method of shared problem solving in which all members of a group spontaneously contribute ideas.

**Conversation:** A spoken exchange of thoughts, opinions, and feelings that is more continuous and sustained than talk.

**Cross-training:** Training employees in skills for more than one job.

**Cross-selling:** Attempting to sell add-ons or accessories with your products and services after a purchase commitment has been made.

**KM channel:** A course or pathway through which information is transmitted and knowledge is exchanged.

**KM Channel Analysis Matrix:** A custom analysis tool designed to identify existing knowledge exchange pathways and brainstorm improvements.

**Mass media:** A means of public communication reaching a large audience.

**Matrix:** An array of elements in row and column form.

**Site histories:** Ongoing log of events and activities related to a particular location.

**Upselling:** Promoting a higher level of product or service after a purchase commitment has been made.

# Developing KM Strategies

*Large organizations, reflectively structured, are well positioned to be highly innovative and deal with discontinuities. If their internal communities have a reasonable degree of autonomy and independence from the dominant world view, large organizations might actually accelerate innovation. Emergent communities that span the boundaries of an organization are likely conduits of external and innovative views into the organization.*

—John Seely Brown, VP and Chief Scientist, Xerox Corp.

*Knowledge is embedded in people, and knowledge creation occurs in the process of social interaction.*

—Karl Erik Sveiby

**Chapter Eleven Learning Objectives**

- ❑ Learn why EVERY project should be considered a KM project.
- ❑ Learn the four key tools that support organizational effectiveness.
- ❑ Introduce the three most common approaches to developing organizational KM strategies.
- ❑ Develop an interest in using metacognitive strategies to improve learning.
- ❑ Understand that thinking styles are situational and open to improvement.

Chapter 10 mentioned a few ways you can improve project management and KM within a team. This is obviously critical when you consider that project management is largely about information management. A project manager is a person who keeps track of time, resources, and functionality-related information either from inception to deployment or through a single project stage. Other key functions include setting expectations and integrating competing goals into a comprehensive strategy.

> **Project manager: A person who manages time, resources, expectations, and functionality-related information either from inception to deployment or through a single project stage.**

The increasing calls for faster, better, and cheaper performance can be extremely hard to accomplish in an environment characterized by operational information silos with duplication of effort, loss of valuable know-how because of turnover, and the tendency to repeat the same mistakes. Knowledge creation, sharing, and use are clearly linked to competitive advantage and meaningful business results. Long-term efforts such as KM call for clearly defined strategies paired with high levels of stakeholder commitment.

Effective knowledge management benefits from a strategic approach, detailed planning, and comprehensive support structures. It does not necessarily require a massive budget, a complete infrastructure change, an army of consultants, and a new software vendor. Many software vendors and IT consultants will push for starting huge KM projects with epic budgets and a rapidly growing number of KM project team members. In fact, there is little need for massive KM projects because, in a sense, every project should be a KM project, especially the massive ones!

Every major corporate project touches on one or more of the following areas:

1. Harmonious interaction throughout the organization (coordination)
2. Facilitating the exchange information (communication)
3. Guiding and supporting the development of effective behaviors (learning)
4. Storing, organizing, and recalling information (memory)

Give these four areas the concern that they deserve in every major project plan.

The logic behind KM is simple to the point of being obvious. It seeks effective gathering and utilization of a company's intellectual capital, both explicit and tacit. Any organization seeking to work more effectively and efficiently, and to deliver the best possible customer service, will need to be sure it is using its knowledge effectively, evolving it constantly, and retaining that knowledge in the face of staff turnover and organizational restructuring. Typically, individuals or organizations use four tools to achieve these goals:

- ❑ Communication
- ❑ Coordination
- ❑ Memory
- ❑ Learning

Obviously, the technologies available to us for improving each of these four areas have improved immensely in the last decade. Although the technologic vision is simple enough, the human tasks are daunting. Immediately, we are faced with the huge and complex areas of individual empowerment, collaborative working, group dynamics, and organizational structures.

In broad terms, KM is about improving the exchange of knowledge held within the individual minds of the employees of an organization. Much of the discussion within KM focuses, quite rightly, on tacit knowledge. It clearly offers the greatest potential for benefit to the bottom line; however, there is also much to consider with regard to documented knowledge (explicit). In fact, the bulk of current technology is focused in this direction.

### Case Study: Developing a KM Strategy

A large energy corporation was concerned with the age of its senior management and the corporation's ability to retain their knowledge. The CEO initiated a knowledge management and succession management initiative to develop a strategy to capture and distribute knowledge to the next generation of senior management.

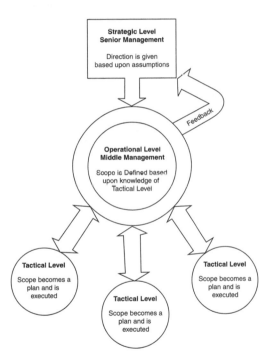

FIGURE 11.1 **Disseminating Information within the Organization.**

The CEO tasked the Senior VP of Learning Leadership and Performance with putting together a multidisciplinary team to develop a strategy for leveraging the corporation's current procedures, processes, and systems to facilitate knowledge management and succession management. The Senior VP put out a call to arms and pulled together a group of approximately 50 individuals from across the corporation who wanted to have input in the design of the strategy. From this group a team of six were selected, five members with voting rights who represented the different stakeholder groups, and a multidisciplinary communications expert to help the team communicate their strategy back to senior management and the corporation.

The team worked for several weeks and developed a strategy that utilized existing procedures and infrastructure to capture the skills that senior management felt would be lost as individuals retired. Following the strategy, potential candidates from within the corporation would then be trained and later screened in their ability to fill future senior roles within the corporation.

The success of the initiative was based on the development of a strategy and high-level plan that utilized communications, procedures, systems, and training for implementation. The project was completed just in time to preserve the company's leadership bench strength during a major restructuring.

New ways of leading, working, and thinking must be practiced until they become habitual. This change is not going to occur all at once across your company. Spreading the ethics of KM throughout your organization will be a long journey. Where to start implementing KM first is a subject that has become increasingly controversial over the last few years. The three most common high-level approaches to developing organizational KM strategies are "top-down," "bottom-up," and "middle-up-down."

## Top-Down KM

Most KM software vendors will recommend a top-down approach. This calls for convincing the most senior members of top-level management first, then the leadership pushes centralized repositories of information, KM tools, and KM technologies downhill to the rest of the company. This strategy is often more effective at selling multimillion-dollar software packages than encouraging any type of collaboration or knowledge sharing because user participation levels are typically very low in these types of systems; however, sometimes the solution a company needs involves a large, high-cost systems implementation, and it will usually have to gain senior management approval and support if it is to be successful.

The problem is that many software vendors tend to paint an elegant, exaggerated, and oversimplified picture of the benefits of implementing KM software. They claim that new software can capture an entire company's documents and e-mail messages and then, simply by applying a common indexing scheme and search functionality, enable anyone to find anything quickly. Of course, there is value in implementing robust search and index functionality, but this type of implementation alone rarely enables companies to manage and leverage the bulk of their intellectual capital assets, and it offers virtually nothing for increasing innovation.

## Bottom-Up KM

Have you ever brought your car to the mechanic because of a strange noise in your engine, only to have it fail to reproduce itself when the mechanic is there? These intermittent problems, an aspect of almost any technology, frustrate everyone involved in the process, are rarely documented, and add costly duplication of effort. Simply capturing fixes to these types of problems and distributing the solutions across the workforce can have a profound performance impact in almost any technical field. Many organizations choose a bottom-up KM strategy to manage these kinds of issues. Bottom-up KM empowers individuals by facilitating personal productivity and collaboration. This is intended to create an enterprise that is better able to capitalize on work already done.

There are many difficulties in deploying KM for an entire organization. It is often much easier to start from the bottom level of an organization. This means starting with deploying KM to smaller parts of the organization and then spreading it further within the company, once the benefits can be easily demonstrated. Accomplishing this goal usually means limiting KM projects to the primary tasks of a department.

In the bottom-up KM model, knowledge sharing begins and ends with the people who have the tactical knowledge. In general, the steps are (1) start with a specific business problem, (2) solve it, (3) show the ROI, and then (4) expand the initiative. Front-line employees are the most immersed in the various organizational processes that make up any business; however, this strategy could lead to a proliferation of segregated silos of information will little capability to integrate, high costs, and high levels of redundancy.

## Middle-Up-Down KM

In Ikujiro Nonaka and Hirotaka Takeuchi's middle-up-down KM model, top management creates the KM vision, while middle management develops more specific initiatives implemented by front-line employees. Managers try to find the middle ground between top management's vision and what is realistically possible within current restraints. Teams provide a forum for sharing the context of information. Individuals can discuss and debate their own perspectives and form new ones. In this strategy, middle managers become the linkages between the ideals of top management and the complex, ever-changing realities of the front-line workers.

Nonaka and Takeuchi view top-down KM strategies as bureaucratic hierarchies that support the collection and application of knowledge, but also limit the individual's initiative and the company's ability to adapt to unexpected, external changes. The bottom-up style of knowledge management promotes individual motivation, as well as the exchange and creation of new knowledge. Unfortunately, the cost is inefficiency in the distribution of newly created knowledge throughout the company because of the temporary nature of project teams.

Another problem with bottom-up KM is that lower-level employees may often lack the ability to see the big picture or may not have the soft skills to communicate the importance of their insights even if they are relevant to the larger business objectives. Many consider the middle-up-down approach to be more focused on explicit knowledge than the top-down KM and more focused on tacit knowledge than the bottom-up approach.

Obviously, the best KM strategy will factor in issues from all levels of an organization. The highest strategic levels of an organization should be expected to agree on and provide an overall *direction*. The next level of operational control should identify valuable *goals* to move the organization in the direction proposed, as well as collecting information from the lower tactical levels of the organization to identify *assumptions, limitations, objectives,* and *measurements* relevant to pursuing those goals. The process depends on open and detailed dialogues with high levels of reflective listening at all ends of the organizational chain.

FIGURE 11.2 **Organizational Knowledge.**

Managers at the operational level should develop KM plans to pursue the direction explicitly identified by the strategic level, based on the explicit input of tactical level knowledge workers. Gathering this information can be quite challenging because of the classic forces that limit dialogue within organizations.

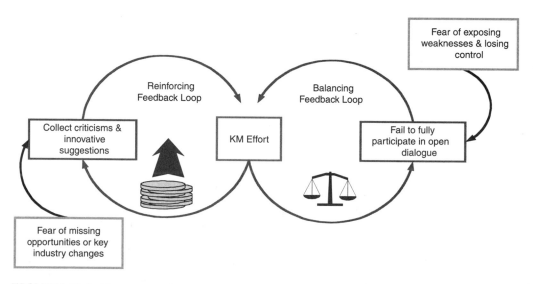

FIGURE 11.3 **How Fear Stalls Many KM Initiatives.** *Note:* Drawing based on techniques described in Peter Senge's book: *The Fifth Discipline.*

In many cases, making internal conversations more explicit can mitigate the fear that stalls KM initiatives. Each level of the organization brings key areas of knowledge to the dialogue. At each level you find new opinions, alternatives, and vested interests, in addition to large areas of ignorance. Avoiding the traditional tribal warfare issues that tend to arise from any new KM-related initiative will require:

1. Establishing a forum for reflective dialogue
2. Explicitly defining goals, assumptions, issues, and limitations
3. Setting expectations well
4. Building success metrics into the plan

### Nonaka's SECI Model

Explicit knowledge is formal, verifiable, and distributable. This makes it much easier to measure, communicate, and share. Tacit knowledge consists of mental models, beliefs, and abstractions that cannot be easily expressed and shared. Nonaka and Takeuchi focus much of their study of innovation on the conversion from personal to organizational knowledge and conversions between explicit and tacit knowledge. Without a store of tacit knowledge, rich in quality, we cannot hope to put together any meaningful explicit knowledge. They contend that equal emphasis must be placed on the entire knowledge conversion process. The process as they see it consists of four key subprocesses: socialization, externalization, combination, and internalization.

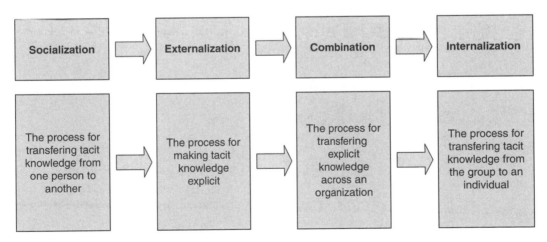

FIGURE 11.4 **The Four Areas of Knowledge Conversion.** Note: Based on Professor Ikujiro Nonaka's SECI Model.

A KM initiative may help communities of practice to get initiated by pushing from the top down, but once initiated they normally self-direct, bring about learning, and improve the practice about which they are organized from the bottom up. Centralized knowledge administration can work for producing higher-value knowledge, but centralized authoring most often results in slowing growth because of the amount of time it takes to make knowledge explicit to a large audience. The wider the range of abstraction levels between individuals, the more time it takes to transfer knowledge.

Unlike information, knowledge is about more than what we know; it is also what we believe in, and it is about commitment and taking action. Information is merely a flow of messages; knowledge is the thing that is created from that flow of information.

> **Knowledge is created via the dynamic interactions between people.**

**In the SECI process, team leaders often play a key role in the collective innovation process and in the process of defining objectives and promoting them to more senior levels in the organization. The aim of the Japanese team leader is to stay focused on delivering the leadership's goals, which are sometimes deliberately ambiguous. They bring together the diverse contributions of the team members to build a cohesive unit. Then the team can make strides of innovation, utilizing the knowledgebase of the whole group. Performed well, this technique delivers extremely powerful results.**

Knowledge leaders in companies focusing on top-down KM often become workflow bottlenecks or gatekeepers. For KM to produce the results that companies are looking for, they will need to put aside their existing command-and-control focus and begin building a culture of collaboration in which everyone is a leader, everyone is learning, and everyone is pursuing higher orders of thinking.

## Thinking about Thinking

Benjamin Bloom created taxonomy for categorizing the level of abstraction of questions and recognizing higher orders of thinking. The taxonomy provides a useful structure in which to categorize test questions because professors often ask questions within particular levels. If you can determine the levels of questions that your instructors habitually use, you will be able to study using the best possible strategies.

Higher-order thinking essentially means thinking that takes place in the higher levels of the hierarchy of cognitive processing. Bloom's taxonomy is the most widely accepted hierarchical arrangement of this sort in the education field, and it can be viewed as a continuum of thinking skills—starting with knowledge-level thinking and moving eventually to evaluation-level of thinking. The need for rapidly evolving learning in organizations demands that we think about how we think; for years psychologists have called this metacognition.

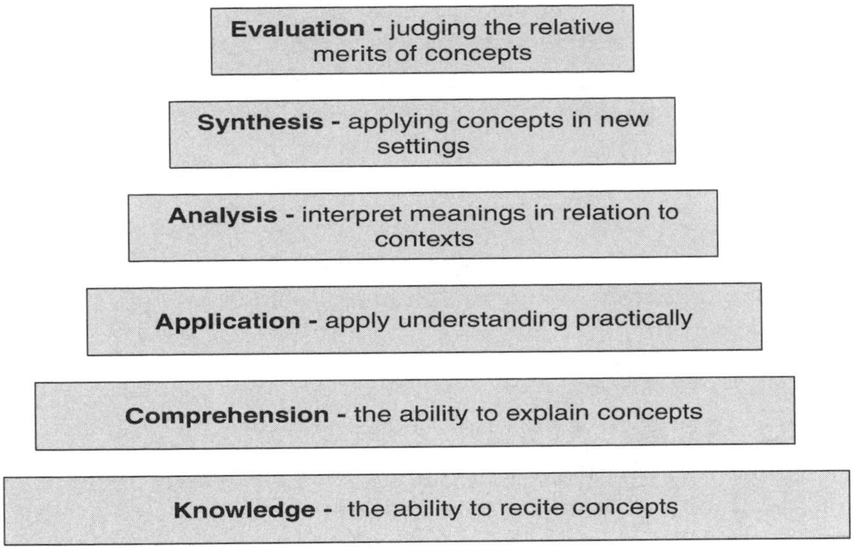

Evaluation - judging the relative merits of concepts

Synthesis - applying concepts in new settings

Analysis - interpret meanings in relation to contexts

Application - apply understanding practically

Comprehension - the ability to explain concepts

Knowledge - the ability to recite concepts

FIGURE 11.5  Bloom's Taxonomy.

## Metacognition

Metacognition refers to a higher order of thought that focuses on active control over cognitive processes. Activities such as planning how to approach a given task, monitoring understanding, and evaluating progress toward the completion of a task are metacognitive in nature. When life presents situations that cannot be handled by learned responses, metacognitive behavior is brought into play. Just as an executive assesses and manages an organization, a thinker must assess and manage his or her thinking style. The basic metacognitive strategies to manage thinking styles are:

1. Connecting new information to existing knowledge, through dialogue

2. Selecting thinking strategies deliberately, with awareness of the alternatives

3. Planning, monitoring, and evaluating thinking processes

Studies show that increases in learning have followed direct instruction in metacognitive strategies. These results suggest that direct teaching of these thinking strategies may be useful, and that independent use develops gradually. (Thomas E. Scruggs et al., "Maximizing what gifted students can learn: Recent findings of learning strategy research," *Gifted Child Quarterly*, 1985;29(4):181–185).

Your thinking strategy is how you gather and process information, make and act on decisions, and even what kind of information you prefer. Like the basic mental models of Chris Argyris and Donald Schön discussed earlier, your thinking strategies will influence your every action. By understanding the thinking styles of yourself and others, you can better understand how to make the most of your interactions.

## Inquiry Modes

The studies of Wes Churchman from the University of California at Berkeley and Ian Miroff from the University of Pittsburgh explored people's "inquiry modes." Inquiry modes represent how people gather and process information. Their studies indicated that people fall into five basic types, based on the thinking strategies they use. Churchman based his taxonomy on the work of noted Western philosophers Kant, Hegel, Singer, Leibniz, and Locke. Later, Alice Kienholz simplified the inquiry modes into realists, idealists, analysts, synthesists, and pragmatists.

## The InQ

The Inquiry Mode Questionnaire (InQ) is a set of statements with forced, multiple-choice responses designed to determine the subject's mode of thinking. You can acquire the InQ for yourself or your organization from InQ Educational Materials, Inc., 640 Davis St., #28, San Francisco, CA 94111; www.inq-hpa.com.

The InQ measures thinking styles and describes the key behavioral cues related to each one. Thinking styles are situational, not functional, and everyone has the opportunity to expand and improve on the thinking styles he or she uses and to better understand the inquiry modes of peers. The products from InQ Educational Materials not only identify preferred thinking styles, but also point toward ways to expand and improve on them. The five thinking styles identified and measured by the InQ are as follows:

**Realists** are inductive and task-oriented. They rely on facts and expert opinion and prefer data to theory. Their mental models are derived chiefly from observation, expert opinion, and their own experience. Their style is empirical. This style is best for well-defined problem situations for which there exists strong consensual position on the nature of the problem. The realist understands the resources that are available and what can be accomplished with them and excels at setting near-term objectives.

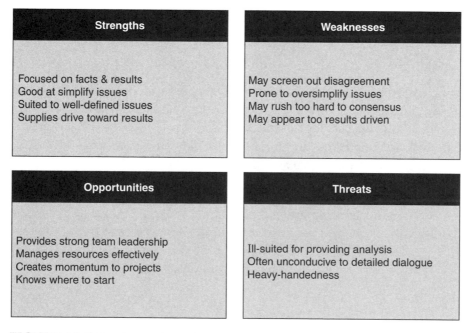

| Strengths | Weaknesses |
|---|---|
| Focused on facts & results<br>Good at simplify issues<br>Suited to well-defined issues<br>Supplies drive toward results | May screen out disagreement<br>Prone to oversimplify issues<br>May rush too hard to consensus<br>May appear too results driven |

| Opportunities | Threats |
|---|---|
| Provides strong team leadership<br>Manages resources effectively<br>Creates momentum to projects<br>Knows where to start | Ill-suited for providing analysis<br>Often unconducive to detailed dialogue<br>Heavy-handedness |

FIGURE 11.6 **Inquiry Mode: Realist.**

**Analysts** see the world as structured, organized, and predictable. They believe there should be one well-planned method for doing anything. Their style is prescriptive and method-oriented, operating with models and formulas. They typically prefer data to theories. If an analyst doesn't feel comfortable about a decision, he or she gathers more data. This style works best for well-structured problems where explicit problem-solving formulas exist. Individuals preferring the realist or analyst inquiry modes typically make excellent stewards.

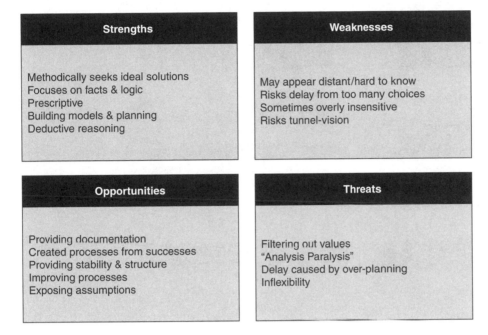

| Strengths | Weaknesses |
|---|---|
| Methodically seeks ideal solutions<br>Focuses on facts & logic<br>Prescriptive<br>Building models & planning<br>Deductive reasoning | May appear distant/hard to know<br>Risks delay from too many choices<br>Sometimes overly insensitive<br>Risks tunnel-vision |

| Opportunities | Threats |
|---|---|
| Providing documentation<br>Created processes from successes<br>Providing stability & structure<br>Improving processes<br>Exposing assumptions | Filtering out values<br>"Analysis Paralysis"<br>Delay caused by over-planning<br>Inflexibility |

FIGURE 11.7  **Inquiry Mode: Analyst.**

**Idealists** welcome a broad range of views. They experience reality as the whole into which new data are assimilated, based on similarities to things they already know. Their style is assimilative, receptive, and need-oriented, assigning equal value to both data and theory. They often listen to intuition rather just relying on the facts. Idealists shun conflict and are always trying to be accommodating. They are better at handling situations that are value-laden.

**Synthesists** focus their thinking on ideas and find connections among things that other people see as having little or no relationship. Their style is challenging, speculative, integrative, and process-oriented. They ask what if and why not, and regard data to be meaningless without interpretation. The ability to look at opposing viewpoints and not pass judgment on them indicates a synthesist preference. Synthesists are skilled at handling controversial issues without discouraging debate and creativity.

**Pragmatists** see the world as constantly changing and largely unpredictable, requiring a flexible, "whatever works" approach to problem solving. Their style is adaptive, incremental, and payoff-oriented. Pragmatists are not ones for great long-range plans and tend to be short-range, practical thinkers. They tend to employ a piecemeal approach to life.

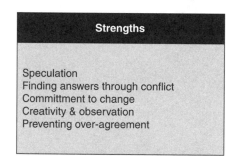

| Strengths | Weaknesses |
|---|---|
| Seeks ideal solutions<br>Sees values inherent in issues<br>Receptive to dialogue<br>Sees the whole picture<br>Humanizes conflicts | May screen out hard data<br>Risks delay from too many choices<br>Sometimes overly sentimental<br>Risks overlooking details |
| **Opportunities** | **Threats** |
| Providing inspirational leadership<br>Encouraging continuity in ethics<br>Articulating values & goals<br>Improving processes & relationships<br>Exposing & challenging assumptions | Potential for ambiguity<br>Fundamentalism<br>Delay caused by over-planning<br>Avoiding conflicts that fuel creativity |

FIGURE 11.8  **Inquiry Mode: Idealist.**

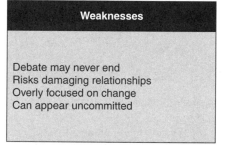
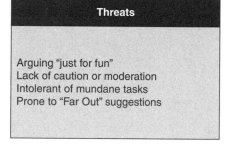

| Strengths | Weaknesses |
|---|---|
| Speculation<br>Finding answers through conflict<br>Committment to change<br>Creativity & observation<br>Preventing over-agreement | Debate may never end<br>Risks damaging relationships<br>Overly focused on change<br>Can appear uncommitted |
| **Opportunities** | **Threats** |
| Illustrating abstract concepts<br>Seeing opportunities for synergy<br>Advocating change<br>Valuable in controversial situations<br>Excellent "Devil's Advocate" | Arguing "just for fun"<br>Lack of caution or moderation<br>Intolerant of mundane tasks<br>Prone to "Far Out" suggestions |

FIGURE 11.9  **Inquiry Mode: Synthesist.**

Because they draw all of the other systems of inquiry into their learning approach, pragmatists are well suited for solving complex issues, but somewhat difficult to identify.

Because each of the five thinking styles is best suited for a particular purpose, it is important to recognize them and have them all readily available for every situation. No individual thinks with purely one style. Most people show preferences for a single

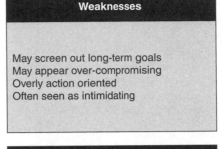

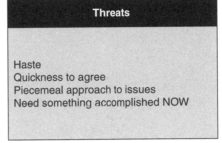

FIGURE 11.10 **Inquiry Mode: Pragmatist.**

style, and some show equal preference for two styles. Just as with individuals, each team, organization, or community should be working to understand its own inquiry modes and the behavioral implications. For example, persons who prefer the analyst and realist inquiry modes will find that accepting diverse dialogue is difficult for them because it requires that they allow the potential for going beyond the information available.

The InQ came about in 1977 when researchers A.F. Harrison, R.M. Bramson, S.J. Bramson, and N. Parlette were asked the question: "How can highly intelligent, experienced managers make absolutely stupid decisions, then push them until a disaster occurs?" Traditional excuses offered include external influences, excessive infighting, lack of vision, or lack of technical know-how in key individuals. Another explanation might be that there is a basic paradox between the objectives of leadership and management. Leadership guru Mel Toomey characterizes the paradox like this: "[M]anagement is focused on reliability, predictability and certainty, whereas leadership is focused on possibility, vision and change."

Organizational conflicts usually seem to come down to two competing camps: (1) those who resist change at the expense of risking stagnation and (2) those who promote change at the expense of devaluing their historic gains. As with most tragic conflicts, both sides are partially right and partially wrong. Solving the paradox of leadership vs. management requires finding ways to facilitate change without sacrificing the gains of the past.

## Additional Learning Resources

- ❑ *Knowledge Emergence: Social, Technical, and Evolutionary Dimensions of Knowledge Creation,* by Ikujiro Nonaka and Toshihiro Nishiguchi, editors (2001)

- ❑ *Taxonomy of Educational Objectives, Handbook 1: Cognitive Domain,* by David Krathwohl and Benjamin S. Bloom (1984)

❑ *The Knowledge-Creating Company,* by Ikujiro Nonaka (1991)

❑ www.dialogonleadership.org/interviewNonaka.html—"Knowledge Has to Do with Truth, Goodness, and Beauty," Interview with Professor Ikujiro Nonaka, February 23, 1996

## Test Your Knowledge

## Discussion Questions

1. What is the role of the project manager?

2. What should you consider when planning a major project?

3. Is technology holding back KM?

4. Pick an organization and then choose a KM implementation strategy that you believe would work within that organization. Why would it work?

5. Determine the levels of test questions that your instructor habitually uses. What is your strategy for studying to gain the best possible test results?

## Review Questions

1. A _____ _____ is a person who keeps track of time, resources, and functionality-related information either from inception to deployment or through a single project stage.

2. Effective knowledge management benefits from a _____ approach, detailed planning, and comprehensive support structures.

3. Although the technological _____ is simple enough, the human tasks are daunting.

4. In broad terms, KM is about improving the _____ of knowledge held within the _____ minds of the employees of an organization.

5. New ways of leading, working, and thinking must be practiced until they become _____.

6. Most KM software vendors will recommend a _____-_____ approach.

7. Bottom-up KM empowers _____ by facilitating personal productivity and collaboration.

8. In Ikujiro Nonaka and Hirotaka Takeuchi's _____-____-_____ KM model, top management creates the KM vision, while middle management develops more specific initiatives implemented by front-line employees.

9. Obviously, the best KM strategy will factor in issues from all levels of an _____.

10. Managers at the _____ _____ level should develop KM plans to pursue the direction explicitly identified by the strategic level, based on the explicit input of tactical-level knowledge workers.

11. _____ knowledge is formal, verifiable, and distributable.

12. Centralized _____ _____ can work for producing higher-value knowledge, but centralized authoring most often results in slowing growth because of the amount of time it takes to make knowledge explicit to a large audience.

13. Bloom's _____ is the most widely accepted hierarchical arrangement of this sort in the education field, and it can be viewed as a continuum of thinking skills—starting with knowledge-level thinking and moving eventually to evaluation-level of thinking.

## Chapter Vocabulary

**Bottom-up KM:** A KM strategy focused on the low-level tactical goals and initiatives that can rapidly produce a strong ROI.

**Communication:** Exchanging information and facilitating dialogue.

**Communities of practice:** A collection of individuals who have an informal relationship based on shared expertise and passion for a particular endeavor.

**Coordination:** Harmonious interaction throughout an organization.

**Group dynamics:** The branch of social psychology that studies the basic nature of groups and how they develop over time.

**Learning:** Acquiring skills to guide and support the development of effective behaviors.

**Memory:** Storing, organizing, and recalling information.

**Metacognition:** A higher order of thought that focuses on active control over cognitive processes.

**Middle-up-down KM:** Ikujiro Nonaka and Hirotaka Takeuchi's KM vision for the definition of roles and responsibilities within the enterprise.

**Reflective dialogue:** Communication technique involving restating and confirming another's person's statements, to ensure proper transfer of information.

**SECI process:** A model of knowledge creation detailing the transformation of knowledge from tacit to explicit.

**Top-down KM:** A KM strategy focused on creating enterprisewide initiatives and pushing them down from the highest levels of authority.

<br>

# Chapter 12

# The Ethics of KM

*Knowledge management is an ongoing, evolutionary process.*
*Once it's part of your business model, it will always be part of*
*your business model.*

—David Keller, Marketing VP at Zoneworx Inc.

## Chapter Twelve Learning Objectives

- ☐ Conversations, rather than personal power games, should be the device for making changes to a company's culture.
- ☐ Individuals approach issues from their own unique worldview and inquiry mode.
- ☐ Ethical landmarks are often built using the cultural institutions of a company.
- ☐ Organizations can use storytelling to give examples of ways that people are demonstrating positive results while operating within ethical boundaries.
- ☐ Innovation and the challenging of old assumptions must be fostered and protected within an organization.
- ☐ Showing tolerance for those with different worldviews and inquiry mode preferences allows the individual or organization to utilize dialogue to build a platform for a stronger and more sustainable future.

In order for individuals to collaborate effectively in any organization, there must be communication and trust. No single mode of inquiry alone can tackle the challenges that modern corporations face. Collaboration and partnerships are required. A comprehensive definition of KM should incorporate the needs and attitudes of people with different temperaments and inquiry modes. The right approach to KM addresses technologic, social, and organizational issues while maintaining a focus on business objectives. KM involves the ethical management of people, not just the efficient distribution of documents.

Through conversations, today's knowledge workers create the relationships that define the effectiveness of their organizations. Conversations, rather than personal power games, should be the device for making changes to a company's culture. Dialogue based on transparent and informed relationships release time and energy for concentrating on business objectives instead of wasting time on confrontations.

Creativity is built into the human condition; it does not require a Harvard MBA to develop. Sometimes it may appear as if one group is obviously more creative than the other, but typically the real difference is in where their creativity is focused. Consider this common double standard, inherent in corporate IT projects.

Imagine a project manager is charged with finding a more efficient procurement process that heavily utilizes Web technology to replace the company's existing solution. The goals might be easier software support, reduced software licensing, and reduced user training as a result of standardizing on a browser interface. The trouble starts when you begin to bring together the team to research the issues and define a strategy. Typically, you will pull together a team with membership from the groups in charge of development, administration, and leadership.

Each of the three groups approaches the issues from its own unique worldview. The development group is expected to be cutting edge. They must constantly explore the latest technologic advances with a mode of analysis that emphasizes a more iterative, prototype-based process. They have their eyes set on the functionality, features, and imperatives of rapidly advancing technology. The administrative group has been tasked with reliability, predictability, and certainty. Their model of analysis includes intensive research, coupled with strictly formalized testing procedures. They focus on performance and scalability issues, as well as what is known from past experiences. The leadership group is usually focused on partnerships, vision, change, and cost controls. They must focus on negotiating a viable path through a chaotic and quickly changing political environment.

Finding an effective strategy that meets the needs and expectations of all three groups, while meeting the key goals of easier software support, reduced software licensing, and reduced user training demands valuing the input of all three groups on the team. Often, this requires upgrading the ethics of the entire team. Valuing human beings is the core of ethics in any environment.

## Ethical Positioning

At some point, it becomes important to stand up and be clear on where you stand in light of ethical issues. When dealing with ethics, there is only right or wrong, but determining your current position during an ethical firestorm can be difficult. What is needed is an ethical global positioning system (GPS), but in absence of such a device, the next best thing is using conventional methods.

Conventional ethical positioning requires similar methods as used by the seafarers of old for determining one's position compared to a fixed object. You must study a fixed object of known ethical position and compare it to where you are on an ethical question to determine which direction will lead you to the truth.

**Example**

A clerk gives you change as if you had given him a $20 bill, when in fact you only gave him $10. Based on the law, the way you are raised, and your faith/beliefs, you should be able to determine that keeping the money you received from the clerk's mistake is wrong. Of course, corporate ethics issues are rarely this simple.

Few startup companies consider how they plan to handle ethics questions; most are concerned with survival rather than accountability. Ethics is considered simple, even though it is not. Consider the vast number of potential ethical threats to a company's sustainability. How dangerous is a worker's tendency to share sexual jokes around the water cooler? Should the company monitor Internet use and e-mail to determine if these activities are causing lost productivity? Criminal activities that could leave the company at risk for both lost profits and future lawsuits begin as complex ethical issues.

**Sustainability: The ability to remain in existence; to be maintainable over the long term.**

The Enron bankruptcy, the largest in U.S. history, wiped out more than $60 billion in stock market value and investors' savings in about one year. Enron's complexity may have outstripped the capacity of its accounting disclosures to convey vital information about its own financial health. The resulting nosedive destroyed Enron and took down Andersen Consulting, Enron's independent auditor, as well. Before the smoke cleared, WorldCom, Qwest Communications, Global Crossing, and several other companies had declared similar lapses in disclosure.

The stock market punished these companies immediately. A crisis of investor confidence consequently erupted that was unrivaled since the Great Depression. Layoffs began sweeping throughout the American technology sector, and employees who had the expectation of career employment suddenly realized they were on their own. As a result, corporate loyalty declined. The heart of the issue was that these companies had booked operating expenses, such as routine maintenance costs, as capital investments, such as buying new operating equipment. This allowed them not only to hide expenses but also to inflate cash flow and report artificial profits. For the short term it worked well, but the expense was their sustainability.

New telecom competitors and the older telephone companies both miscalculated how fast demand for their capacity was growing. In building and upgrading their networks, they had sunk billions into new technology only to see new advancements leapfrog their efforts. Not only did they miss the fact that telecom prices and profits were dropping at an unusually high pace, but they also continued to rack up debt that was backed up by obsolete assets. Looking back at the total damage caused by the accounting scandals of 2002, it is shocking to think that so much accounting money could be spent to return so little accountability.

A lot of decisions are not easily made, but the correct direction does exist; sometimes it may simply require greater examination and analysis to determine it. As an organization, it is vital that landmarks, fences, and demilitarized zones (DMZs) are used as boundaries to help members of that organization determine quickly and easily that they are on the correct side of organizational policy and to help make ethical issues clear. For the sake of scope we are limiting our focus of ethics to organizational ethics; ethics dealing with personal freedoms fall outside of our discussion.

## Landmarks, Fences, and DMZs

As companies grow and drive toward increased profitability, the methods they use for reporting become more complex. This complexity makes it more difficult to determine where the ethical line falls. Because this complexity exists, companies need to use policies, procedures, and communications to clearly mark where the ethical line lies.

Some issues within a company can be identified easily by using a landmark. We use the term *landmark* to represent high-level ethical guidelines. These issues typically are not extremely complex, and a simple landmark as a warning is all that is required to protect the honest. Typically, a landmark sets far enough back from the ethical line that a slight straying past the landmark does not put the individual or group in immediate danger of crossing the ethical line.

Ethical landmarks are often built using the company's culture. For example, many companies now value the demonstration of social responsibility among their employees. To encourage behavior consistent with this value, organizations often promote things such as recycling waste, donating to local charities, or paying employees to work in community events. Another way companies build an ethical culture is through storytelling; a good example of this is the grocery store chain case study from Chapter 6.

Working with KM consultants from IBM Global Services, the company developed a story about a customer who had dropped her grocery bags on the ground after checking out. The story described an employee's response, which got him a reward for extraordinary customer service. In the Chapter 6 case study, the KM consultants from IBM helped the corporation develop a word-of-mouth way of delivering the story and monitoring its movement throughout the corporation. Other ways a company can disseminate positive cultural stories are through company newsletters, global e-mail messages, and intranet sites.

Major ethical problems occur when there are significant value conflicts among differing interests, real alternatives that are all equality justifiable, and/or dire consequences to stakeholders in the situation. Fences, to keep anyone from accidentally crossing, should mark issues that fall much closer to the ethical line. A *fence* is an explicit boundary that shows exactly where an important ethical line lies. Most official company ethics policies fall under the category of fences. That fence must be crossed in order to stray beyond the right side of ethics.

Policies and procedures are the corporation's ethical fences and should therefore be more than merely accessible and understandable: they should be ubiquitous. Organizations can use storytelling to give examples of ways that people are demonstrating positive results while operating within the ethical fence. Storytelling can also help employees understand the policy and why it exists. The policies define the fence and the procedures define operating within the limits of the ethical fence.

Some issues are so explosive that it is wise for a company to construct a DMZ to ensure that crossing the ethical line requires great effort and that anyone who does cross the line can be discovered. DMZs are established when the cost of continuing conflict exceeds the potential value of resolution or resolution is extremely unlikely. DMZs are distinguished from fences by active compliance monitoring.

In the world of KM and ethics, DMZs can be represented by automated systems, such as the monitoring of software licenses being handled involuntarily and reporting when a company is nearing their limits. Procedures can also be made to be sufficiently strict that they can be used in the company's DMZ. Requiring that all calls to your company's ethics hotline be documented and investigated is a good way to ensure that violators are exposed and dealt with appropriately.

TABLE 12.1 **Landmarks, Fences, and DMZs**

| Landmarks | Fences | DMZs |
|---|---|---|
| Gives a general idea of where ethical line is | Defines exactly where the ethical line is | Defines exactly where the ethical line is |
| Does not impede employee from crossing ethical line | Actively discourages employees from crossing ethical lines | Prevents employees from crossing ethical lines |
| Does not monitor violations of ethical line | Does not monitor all violations of ethical line | Monitors and reports violations of ethical line |

Corporate policies can be effective in static environments that see little change over time. Times and situations will eventually change to force employees to make ethical choices that are not addressed in the corporate policies. As our relationships with customers, vendors, and partners take on more complexity, the need for employees to make their own judgment calls increases. At times like these, we are forced to let our conscience guide us.

## Evaluating Situational Ethics

Table 12.2 is designed to help you clarify your ethical perspective when making tough ethical choices.

For each of the seven considerations, choose yes, no, or maybe. For each "yes" answer, count two points; for each "no" answer, count zero points; and for each "maybe" answer, count only one point. The higher scores of 15–21 indicate a strong level of confidence in your choice; midrange scores of 10–14 indicate reluctance to pursue your choice; and lower scores of 0–13 indicate that the ethics of this choice worries you. This table will

TABLE 12.2  **Evaluating Situational Ethics**

| Factor | Consideration | Rating |
|---|---|---|
| **Involvement** | Have I involved all of the stakeholders' viewpoints in my thought process? | Yes  No  Maybe |
| **Fairness** | If I took the place of my stakeholders, would I see this decision as essentially fair? | Yes  No  Maybe |
| **Consequences** | Have I considered the consequences of this decision? | Yes  No  Maybe |
| **Relevance** | Have I gathered as much information as possible to make an informed decision? | Yes  No  Maybe |
| **Values** | Does this decision uphold my personal values? | Yes  No  Maybe |
| **Community** | Would I want this decision to become a global law applicable to all similar situations? | Yes  No  Maybe |
| **Shame** | How would I feel if the details of this decision and action plan were disclosed for all to know? | Yes  No  Maybe |

not tell you right from wrong, but it can help you understand why a choice is causing you worry.

# Managing Ethical Liabilities

In the event of an ethical lapse, ethics management programs and cooperation with authorities can lower potential fines by as much as 80%. In fact, the *only* way an organization can lower its liability to potential fines *before* an ethics violation occurs is to create an effective ethics management program. Such a program must be directed at preventing, detecting, and reporting ethics violations.

Companies are expected to promote ethical behavior in four key areas:

1. *Prevention.* Codes of conduct, statements of business, or standard operating practices help prevent ethical lapses by providing landmarks, fences, and DMZs to help simplify complex interactions. Honor the past by communicating successes and actions that promote your company's values.

2. *Detection.* Automation and integrated systems can be set up to help enforce sharing key information and monitoring ethical compliance. Implement systems that maintain your standards as well as verify the appropriate control and use of company assets.

3. *Reporting.* All companies should have an ethics reporting system in which employees can report criminal conduct by others or receive guidance in solving ethical issues. Training and communications should be used to ensure that employees are aware of the ethical reporting options available to them. Reports should be handled as confidentially as possible, and employees should suffer NO retaliation for ethics reports made in good faith.

4. *Investigation.* Unfortunately, no matter how good an organization's defenses are, not all theft and fraud can be identified and stopped. Within the corporate environment, it is generally accepted that ethical offenses are increasing, and employers need proof to take decisive action. When a potential ethical violation is brought to light within the company, the prudent course is to investigate the alleged conduct to determine whether a violation has in fact occurred and to collect data to inform decisions regarding remedial actions. Because of the controversial nature of these investigations, outside assistance is often brought in to provide thoroughness, fairness, and neutrality.

## Values and KM

The previous sections discussed why KM landmarks, fences, and DMZs should be used to track, protect, and promote ethics and values; however, too strong of a focus on monitoring and regulation can lead to a lack of innovation. KM principles can help protect and promote values and ethics, but that is not the end of the cycle. It is also important to realize that values and ethics can be used to promote and protect KM.

Innovation and challenging old assumptions must be fostered and protected within an organization. People who innovate need to be recognized and rewarded as a normal part of the organization's activities. Building an environment that promotes and rewards individuals for innovation increases an organization's opportunities for knowledge exchange, but it should not be allowed to come at the expense of ethics or business sustainability.

> *"One of the great dangers of knowledge management technology is that it can lead you to invest in systems for reusing knowledge when innovation is central to your company's value proposition."*
>
> —Thomas A. Stewart, *The Case Against Knowledge Management,*
> www.business20.com/articles/mag/0,1640,36747,FF.html

Actions dealing with extremely controversial, high-impact issues like ethics are always at risk of suffering from bias. Triangulation is the application and combination of several inquiry methodologies in the study of the same issue. Combining multiple observers, theories, archetypes, and inquiry modes helps overcome intrinsic biases and the other problems that come from the single-inquiry method, single-observer, and single-theory research.

> **Triangulation: The application and combination of several inquiry methodologies in the study of the same issue.**

Experts and novices perceive information differently, remember it differently, and use different criteria to determine the relevance of the information that they perceive and remember. Although experts are equipped with an extensive knowledge of domain-specific information, they are also prone to developing automatic behavior responses, meaning that they look at events as typical and appropriate solutions as obvious. This accounts for the speed at which the experts are able to diagnose problems and provide specific corrective feedback, but it also illustrates how experts and the organizations that they belong to can get stuck in a rut. The following story describes the process that causes bad ideas to endure; you will often see this story under the title of "How Company Policy Is Made."

### Case Study: Five Monkeys in a Cage (Where Best Practices Go When They Die)

Start with a cage containing five monkeys. In the cage, hang a banana on a string and put a set of stairs under it. Soon, a monkey will go to the stairs and start to climb toward the banana. As soon as he touches the stairs, spray all of the monkeys with cold water.

After a while, another monkey will make an attempt to get the banana; when he does, repeat the previous action and spray all of the monkeys with cold water. Pretty soon, when a third monkey tries to climb the stairs, the other monkeys will move to prevent it.

Now, turn off the cold water. Remove one monkey from the cage and replace it with a new one. The new monkey will see the banana and naturally begin to climb the stairs. To his horror, all of the other monkeys attack him! After another attempt and attack, he knows that if he tries to climb the stairs, he will be assaulted.

Next, remove one more of the original five monkeys and replace it with a new one. The newcomer will go to the stairs and subsequently get attacked. Surprisingly, the previous newcomer takes part in the punishment with enthusiasm. Again, replace a third original monkey with a new one. The new one makes it to the stairs and is attacked as well. Remember that two of the four monkeys that beat the newest monkey have no idea why they were not permitted to climb the stairs or why they are participating in the beating of the newest monkey.

Finally, replace the fourth and fifth original monkeys. Now the monkeys that were originally sprayed with cold water have all been replaced. Nevertheless, no monkey ever again approaches the stairs. Why not?

### "Because that's the way it's always been around here."

Triangulation is a tool for directly assessing the reliability and validity data. It can provide an effective defense against getting trapped into obsolete policies, but it requires accepting and honoring worldviews that are different from your own. It should be a regular part of your critical thinking toolbox.

Tolerance is another key part of developing a KM perspective on ethics. As stated at the beginning of this chapter, "Valuing human beings is the core of ethics." A corporation, like an ecosystem, consists of a diverse array of unique entities all competing for limited resources. Showing tolerance and eventually honoring those with different worldviews and inquiry mode preferences allows the individual or organization to utilize dialogue to build a platform for a stronger and more sustainable future.

**Additional Learning Resources**

- ❑ *The Wealth of Knowledge: Intellectual Capital and the Twenty-first Century Organization,* by Thomas A. Stewart (2001)

- ❑ *Do Business with People You Can Trust: Balancing Profits and Principles,* by L. J. Rittenhouse (2002)

- ❑ *Enron: The Rise and Fall,* by Loren Fox (2002)

- ❑ *Liberating the Corporate Soul: Building a Visionary Organization,* by Richard Barrett (1998)

- ❑ *Bringing Your Soul to Work: An Everyday Practice,* by Cheryl Peppers and Alan Briskin (2000)

 **Test Your Knowledge**

## Discussion Questions

1. What is required to have open dialogue?

2. Are ethics important to KM? Why?

3. How does technology affect ethics and KM?

4. How do you plan to protect yourself and your organization from making poor ethical decisions?

5. How does sustainability affect ethics? Give an example.

Review Questions

1. In order for individuals to _____ effectively in any organization, there must be communication and trust.

2. A comprehensive _____ of KM should incorporate the needs and attitudes of people with different temperaments and inquiry modes.

3. _____, rather than personal power games, should be the device for making changes to a company's culture.

4. When dealing with ethics, there is only right or wrong, but determining your current _____ during an ethical firestorm can be difficult.

5. A lot of decisions are not easily made, but the correct direction does exist; sometimes it may simply require greater _____ and analysis to determine it.

6. As an organization, it is vital that landmarks, fences, and demilitarized zones (DMZs) are used as _____ to help members of that organization determine quickly and easily that they are on the correct side of organizational policy and to help make ethical issues clear.

7. These issues typically are not extremely complex, and a simple landmark as a _____ is all that is required to protect the honest.

8. Ethical _____ are often built using the culture of a company.

9. Another way companies build an ethical culture is through _____ _____; a good example of this is the grocery store chain case study from Chapter 6.

10. Major ethical problems occur when there are significant value conflicts among differing interests, real alternatives that are all equality justifiable, and/or dire consequences to _____ in the situation.

11. A fence is an explicit _____ that shows exactly where an important ethical line lies.

12. Some issues are so _____ that it is wise for a company to construct a DMZ to ensure that crossing the ethical line requires great effort and that anyone who does cross the line can be discovered.

13. In the world of KM and ethics, DMZs can be represented by automated systems, such as the monitoring of software licenses being handled _____ and reporting when a company is nearing their limits.

14. In the event of an ethical lapse, ethics management programs and cooperation with authorities can lower potential _____ by as much as 80%.

15. KM principles can help protect and promote values and ethics, but that is not the end of the _____.

16. Building an _____ that promotes and rewards individuals for innovation increases an organization's opportunities for knowledge exchange, but it should not be allowed to come at the expense of ethics or business _____.

17. Triangulation is the application and combination of several inquiry _____ _____ in the study of the same issue.

18. Experts and novices _____ information differently, remember it differently, and use different criteria to determine the relevance of the information that they perceive and remember.

19. _____ is a tool for directly assessing the reliability and validity data.

20. Tolerance is a key part of developing a _____ perspective on ethics.

21. Showing tolerance and eventually honoring those with different worldviews and _____ mode preferences allows the individual or organization to utilize dialogue to build a platform for a stronger and more sustainable future.

## Chapter Vocabulary

**Accountability:** Responsibility to someone or for some activity.

**Critical thinking:** A cognitive process based on reflective thought and a tolerance for ambiguity.

**Demilitarized zones (DMZs):** Systems, often automated, that seek to prevent a company's employees from crossing ethical lines.

**Fences:** Policies and procedures that show employees clear ethical lines to avoid crossing.

**Iterative:** Characterized by or involving repetition, recurrence, reiteration, or repetitiousness.

**Landmarks:** High-level ethical guidelines that point out areas where employees approach ethical lines.

**Sustainability:** The ability to remain in existence; to be maintainable over the long term.

**Tolerance:** Willingness to recognize and respect the beliefs or practices of others.

**Triangulation:** The application and combination of several inquiry methodologies in the study of the same issue.

**Chapter**

**13**

# Metrics and Taming Wicked Problems

*Some problems are so complex that you have to be highly intelligent and well informed just to be undecided about them.*

—Laurence J. Peter

**Chapter Thirteen Learning Objectives**

- ❑ Be aware that choosing the wrong metrics, or misconstruing their relevance, risks allowing your metrics to cost you your objectives.

- ❑ Know that advocating knowledge sharing as the normal way of doing business can sometimes increase the difficulty of inquiring into the impact of those particular KM projects.

- ❑ Learn the difference between "complicated" and "complex" systems.

- ❑ Recognize that wicked environments can be incrementally improved upon, but rarely (if ever) will an ideal "solution" be found.

I t is not enough to collect a database full of information and hope people begin to use it and contribute knowledge. After establishing a centralized knowledgebase in an easily accessible place, it becomes time to evaluate its performance. Typically, performance metrics are anecdotal, quantitative, or qualitative, but how can you measure such intangibles as communication, collaboration, and trust?

**Anecdotal metrics:** Measures based on casual observations or indications rather than rigorous analysis. This type of analysis is often used to measure the dissemination of certain stories, values, and ideas throughout an organization.

**Quantitative metrics:** Measures that determine amount or quantity. The measurement of the time required to capture the information in a usable manner provides a useful metric for evaluating and improving data capture operations. The level of knowledgebase authoring is often used to measure acceptance and buy-in for KM initiatives.

**Qualitative metrics:** Measures of, relating to, or concerning quality. Qualitative measures are inherently subjective. Examples include feedback measurement systems such as amazon.com's book-rating system or a "thumbs-up or thumbs-down" method of capturing the value of a tip to a user. Other measurements can be made using the number of times a lesson was used or through a system that captures users comments.

## Measurement Stages

At the beginning of any KM measurement program, the focus is usually on inputs (money and labor), tasks (dialogue, design, and development) and timeframes. Because most management initiatives are driven by financial results, the instinct will be to identify classic financial measurements, such as productivity increases, sales improvements, and cost reductions. KM projects will rarely be able to directly generate these financial statistics in their early stages.

Later, the focus of measurement will shift to outputs (reports, statistics, processes, and products) and results (culture, cash, and client satisfaction). Finding correlations between inputs and results is particularly difficult in a corporate environment. The perceived utility of metrics comes from how well they are tied to general business objectives. They are primarily useful for two things: inquiry and advocacy.

A CEO may measure success based on such things as market opinion, employee productivity, and profits (goal: higher stock price). Project managers may tend to measure instead the progress made in developing buy-in and support for their initiative (goal: rapid project completion). Consultants often focus on what projects they have sold to other companies to leverage knowledge sharing (goal: sell more consulting). When considering KM metrics, you should make sure to consider the source of any suggestions before judging their relevance.

> Choosing the wrong metrics, or misconstruing their relevance, risks allowing your metrics to cost you your objectives. Gaining an understanding of what your suppliers, customers, and peer companies are doing to enable knowledge sharing is a good idea, but it doesn't necessarily provide a viable path for your organization. Take care that your metrics do not overemphasize any one group's issues.

## The Paradox within KM Metrics

KM measuring strategies come with a built-in paradox. The more success a company has in advocating knowledge sharing as the normal way of doing business, the more difficult it will be to inquire into the effect of any particular actions or expenditures in knowledge management. Also, if the KM measurement is seen as time-consuming and futile, this can result in people avoiding the effort of sharing knowledge just to avoid the complex measurement. The measures of inputs, tasks, outputs, and results can go a long way toward reassuring skeptics that your KM program is progressing. But to keep your funding alive, you will probably need to create layers of metrics that tie individual employee contributions to senior management initiatives.

The budgetary and resource competition constraints faced by departments within corporations add to the "wickedness" of implementing an enterprise KM system. Horst Rittel, a pioneering theorist of design and planning, authored the seminal work on the complex nature of design and planning problems. He coined the term "wicked problems" to contrast with "tame problems" such as mathematics or chess. Rittel's ideas were later updated and expanded on by Dr. Jeff Conklin.

### Tame Problems vs. Wicked Problems

One of the main obstacles in KM implementations is the fact that knowledge management problems are wicked. According to Conklin, wicked problems have several defining characteristics:

1. You cannot understand the problem until you have offered and perhaps even prototyped a solution.
2. The stakeholders have radically differing worldviews, and thus differing abstractions.
3. The problem-solving process is tightly constrained by things such as deadlines, budgets, team membership, and so on, and the constraints keep changing.
4. The issues are open-ended, never to be solved in the traditional sense.

Large organizations of free-thinking, different-minded individuals always struggle with finding shared understanding and commitment. The inherent diversity of thought, experience, and opinion that is found in any corporation is both the source of internal conflict and the engine for creativity and innovation. Enterprise systems have reached such a level of complexity that no individual can possibly know all of the relevant facts involved in their implementation, impact, and upkeep. To overcome the limitations of individual knowledge, companies may need to evolve more decentralized mechanisms for transmitting and validating information.

# Classic Problem Solving

The scientific method offers the classic academic problem-solving approach: define the problem, gather observational data, analyze the data, formulate a solution, and implement the solution. For clear-cut, unconstrained, and easily understood problems, this works great. In the past, this linear approach was thought to be effective no matter how difficult the problem. In fact, the conventional wisdom often held that the more difficult the problem, the more important it was to follow this highly structured process. Surprisingly, people rarely solve wicked issues in this linear fashion.

To understand why, you need to have a clear knowledge of the difference between complex and complicated. A complicated system may be very large. It may take more than a lifetime to learn the functions of every part of the system, but it is essentially predictable.

Complicated systems are completely definable by strict rules of operation. Automobiles have grown very complicated over the years, but they are still merely the sum of their parts.

Complex systems have inherently unpredictable balancing and reinforcing loops in them. In contrast to complicated systems, they include self-directing elements with dynamic interactions. An election is complex because of the inability to predict how individuals will act. Difficulty in calculation should not be confused with dynamic complexity. Complicated problems can usually be solved by the linear application of carefully defined procedures. Typically, it takes an opportunity-driven process that is much more iterative than the classic scientific method to solve the most complex issues.

> **In fact for the biggest, most wicked issues, even science doesn't rely on linear methods.**

Consider the complex nature of the international scientific community. The body of scientific knowledge created by this community is made up of theories, experiments, observations, and so on conducted by independent researchers all over the world. They work under no centralized authority to bind them all together, yet they have created a unified body of work of amazing breadth and complexity. The thing that distinguishes this unplanned body of work from a quagmire of separate and disconnected thoughts is the emerging structure that has spontaneously evolved. The keys to its success are transparency and self-correcting procedures.

The many individuals, scientific associations, academic journals, and colleges that make up the various elements of the scientific community are all in constant communication. Through Websites, newsgroups, conferences, journals, letters, and countless other forums, scientists connect, collaborate, criticize, and peer review. No resources are applied to reducing duplication of effort or realignment to focus on core competencies. Individual scientists choose their own projects. Geniuses are applauded and scoundrels are exposed, all to support two primary goals: (1) to transmit valid information in a decentralized way and (2) ensure the sustainability of the network.

## Wicked Problem Solving

Famed Austrian economist Friedrich von Hayek distinguished between two kinds of problem-solving processes: constructive rationalism and evolutionary rationalism. In *constructive rationalism*, the problem-solving process is based on known facts and linear logic. *Evolutionary rationalism* becomes applicable when all of the facts are unavailable and the problems go beyond the ability of simple logic to solve. In solving wicked problems, the solution of one aspect of the problem often reveals (or creates) another, more complex problem.

Constructive rationalism represents the view that rational actions are determined entirely by known and demonstrable truths. Evolutionary rationalism recognizes that many problems must be dealt with without the comfort of known and demonstrable truths. It relies on adaptive, opportunity-driven processes that use feedback and dialogue to sort out desirable practices and outcomes over time. Adaptive processes are nothing new; they've been used successfully in design organizations for decades. Most public and business policy is developed in this manner, as are most marketing and process-control systems.

The more adaptive problem-solving method of evolutionary rationalism calls for setting a general target and using feedback to refine both the target and the process as learning takes place. Understanding of the problem continues to evolve as long as the project continues. For instance, when bringing up a new product manufacturing line, a series of designed experiments, along with adaptive process-control algorithms, may be used to establish and continually fine-tune device settings, environmental conditions, and production rates. Each iteration of the process leads to incremental improvement and better understanding of the issues involved, while maintaining the option to roll back changes that cause unacceptably negative side effects.

The development of mechanisms to support effective information sharing and open dialogue are both necessary conditions for effective utilization of evolutionary rationalism. Whether you call it "double-loop learning," "adaptive processes," or "evolutionary rationalism," the bottom line is that wicked problems should be dealt with by absorbing a more complex mass of information than we are used to dealing with, while unleashing group creativity, team learning, and opportunity-driven thinking. In this way, we can incrementally improve wicked environments, but rarely (if ever) will an ideal solution be found.

## Taming the Wicked Problem

It is possible—in fact, easy—to tame a wicked problem. To do so, you simply construct a problem definition that obscures the wicked nature of the problem and then apply linear methods to solving it. This is a deceptively simplistic technique that is all too common in large organizations. Here is how it works.

Suppose we are trying to decide whether to integrate a newly purchased company's ERP system into the existing enterprise business processes or to migrate the new company's data into the purchasing company's system. In order to deliver the project within the deadline set by management, we base our decision on an analysis of implementation costs and a comparison matrix showing each system's functionality. Because process is so confusing and time consuming, we ignore peripheral system effects, training needs, vendor issues, and the effect on upcoming projects. We have tamed the problem and can make a decision on time. Of course, we have merely shifted the burden of the most complex issues to other teams and departments.

### Five Taming Techniques for Wicked Problems

1. *Redefine the problem.* Reduce the problem definition to include only a subcomponent of the larger issue. For instance, when facing an extremely wicked problem, one may

simply redefine it as a research issue. This reduces the objectives of the project to analysis and documentation, postponing any actual movement toward a solution—perhaps indefinitely.

2. *Declare victory.* Through the wholesale application of authority, it is possible to declare the problem solved, end the discussion, and then move on to other more tame issues. When faced with a costly and expensive invasion of Great Britain, Adolph Hitler stood on the cliffs overlooking the English Channel and declared Britain defeated. Similar to his halt in France before destroying or capturing Britain's expeditionary force at Dunkirk, Hitler declared victory only to be later haunted by "ghost" soldiers. Declaring victory doesn't cause the problem to go away; it postpones the inevitable.

3. *Rig the metrics.* Count only the things you can show improvement on and then let the measurement equal the problem. Improving your company's "bench strength" can be a very wicked problem. Often, hiring and recruiting incentives can have a negative (balancing loop) effect on existing employee retention. By tracking only the number of new candidates interviewed and hired, you can ignore employee retention issues and significantly reduce the scope of your issues.

4. *Stay in your foxhole.* Do your job, but take no chances or make no serious effort/investment in actually solving the problem. Hope it goes away. Reduce the problem to the simple issue of following the orders you are given.

5. *Go shopping.* Consider a small group of products as possible solutions to the problem and then reduce the problem into choosing which product to purchase. It is infinitely easier to decide whether to buy PeopleSoft or SAP's Enterprise Resource Planning product than it is to solve the terribly wicked problems associated with the distribution of resources within an organization.

TABLE 13.1 **Taming Wicked Problems Matrix**

| Issue | Wicked Problem? | Tame Problem? | How Could Problem Be Tamed? |
|---|---|---|---|
| Reducing crime in our city. | Yes | | Rig the metrics by decriminalizing certain common crimes and declare victory when the arrest rate drops. |
| Choosing the best enterprise software to support your business. | Yes | | Redefine the problem to choosing the cheapest ERP system . . . then do the math. |
| Replacing a faulty component in a system. | | Yes | |
| Choosing what you want to eat for lunch. | | Yes | |
| Designing a new global procurement system. | Yes | | Redefine the problem to choosing a new procurement software package and go shopping! |

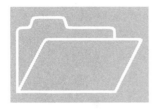

### Case Study: Taming a Wicked ERP Problem

Some problems at first pass do not seem wicked until you look beneath the surface. This was the case when a large corporation decided to consolidate their enterprise resource planning (ERP) systems from twelve systems to one. It's easy to see how one person's common sense solution was actually a very wicked problem.

A large conglomerate had 12 operating companies that were all using different ERPs. Each company had chosen a different ERP vendor or a set of system customizations that they thought best supported their business processes. Senior management in the corporation believed that this situation represented an opportunity to improve reporting and reduce support costs. To this end, an initiative was created to investigate what it would take to convert to one ERP system.

The team met for months gathering, discussing, and analyzing information. The user community became worried and upset that there would be lost functionality. The systems development groups had invested much time and effort into their existing ERP customizations and were less than enthusiastic to abandon them. Management within some groups became concerned that they would be strapped with the costs from another corporate synergy fiasco.

From this entanglement stepped forth a small group with a plan to tame the wicked problem. They defined the wicked problem as: "The applying of one ERP system to multiple extremely different business units." The group approached senior management with questions about the project's objectives. They quickly found that there were two main objectives: consolidating reporting into a more manageable form and reducing cost.

With this refined scope, the small team addressed the wicked problem with the idea of taming it, not solving it. They realized that no single system would meet each company's existing needs, so they redefined the problem. By reorganizing the businesses, three ERP systems could be used to meet each company's existing needs while achieving the root objectives of lowering costs and improving reporting. Combining operating companies into three silos rather than twelve different operating companies, with vastly different business processes, met the senior management's objectives with less risk to the overall corporation. The end result was strong reporting and a huge reduction in costs. These results would not have been achieved by simply focusing on reducing the ERP vendors.

**The best method for dealing with a wicked problem is to focus on incremental improvement and meeting the core objectives. Beware of "common sense" approaches to achieve "quick solutions."**

### Additional Learning Resources

- ❑ "Dilemmas in a General Theory of Planning," by H. Rittel and M. Webber, *Policy Sciences*, 1973;4:155–169

- ❑ *The Art of Systems Thinking: Essential Skills for Creativity and Problem Solving*, by Joseph O'Connor and Ian McDermott (1997)

❑ *The New Organizational Wealth: Managing & Measuring Knowledge-Based Assets*, by Karl Erik Sveiby (1997)

❑ *Law, Legislation and Liberty: The Political Order of a Free People*, by Friedrich A. Hayek (1981)

❑ *If Only We Knew What We Know: The Transfer of Internal Knowledge and Best Practice*, by Carla S. O'Dell et al. (1998)

❑ *Systems Thinking: Managing Chaos and Complexity: A Platform for Designing Business Architecture*, by Jamshid Gharajedaghi (1999)

❑ *The Manager's Pocket Guide to Systems Thinking*, by Stephen G. Haines (1999)

❑ *Facilitating Organization Change: Lessons from Complexity Science*, by Edwin E. Olson, Glenda H. Eoyang, Richard Beckhard, and Peter Vaill (2001)

 **Test Your Knowledge**

## Discussion Questions

1. Name three wicked problems that are commonly in the news.

2. Can you think of some ways leaders have tried to tame these wicked problems?

3. How can improved metrics result in creating new wicked problems?

4. What difficulties arise when trying to measure KM initiatives?

5. What is the difference between a tame problem and a wicked problem?

## Review Questions

1. Typically, _____ metrics are anecdotal, quantitative, or qualitative, but how can you measure such intangibles as communication, collaboration, and trust?

2. Measures relating quality are called _____ measures.

3. At the beginning of any KM _____ program, the focus is usually on inputs (money and labor), tasks (dialogue, design, and development) and timeframes.

4. Finding _____ between inputs and results is particularly difficult in a corporate environment.

5. When considering KM metrics, consider the _____ of any suggestions.

6. Choosing the wrong metrics, or misconstruing their _____, risks allowing your metrics to cost you your objectives.

7. The more success a company has in _____ knowledge sharing, as the normal way of doing business, the more difficult it will be to _____ into the effect of any particular actions or expenditures in knowledge management.

8. Horst Rittel, a pioneering theorist of design and planning, authored the seminal work on the _____ _____ of design and planning problems.

9. The inherent diversity of thought, experience, and opinion that is found in any corporation is both the source of internal _____ and the engine for _____ and innovation.

10. The _____ method offers the classic academic problem-solving approach: define the problem, gather observational data, analyze the data, formulate a solution, and implement the solution.

11. The body of knowledge created by the scientific community is made up of theories, experiments, observations, and so on conducted by _____ researchers all over the world.

12. Famed Austrian _____ Friedrich von Hayek distinguished between two kinds of problem-solving processes: constructive rationalism and evolutionary rationalism.

13. _____ rationalism recognizes that many problems must be dealt with without the comfort of known and demonstrable truths.

14. The more adaptive problem-solving method of evolutionary rationalism calls for setting a general target and using _____ to refine both the target and the process as learning takes place.

15. Whether you call it "double-loop learning," "adaptive processes," or "evolutionary rationalism," the bottom line is that wicked problems should be dealt with by _____ a more complex mass of information than we are used to dealing with, while unleashing group creativity, team learning, and opportunity-driven thinking.

16. The best method for dealing with a wicked problem is to focus on _____ improvement and meeting the core objectives. Beware of common sense approaches to achieve quick solutions.


## Chapter Vocabulary

**Anecdotal metrics:** Measurements based on casual observations or indications rather than rigorous analysis.

**Complex systems:** Systems having inherently unpredictable balancing and reinforcing loops in them. They include self-directing elements with dynamic interactions that make them unfractionable, unpredictable, and essentially more than the sum of their parts.

**Complicated systems:** Difficult to analyze, yet ultimately predictable, systems containing intricately combined or involved components.

**Constructive rationalism:** A linear problem-solving process based on known facts and step-by-step logic.

**Evolutionary rationalism:** A problem-solving method based on adaptive, opportunity-driven techniques such as prototyping.

**Qualitative metrics:** Measurements of, relating to, or concerning quality.

**Quantitative metrics:** Measurements that determine amount or quantity.

**Wicked problems:** Complex issues where each attempt to create a solution changes the understanding of the problem.

**Chapter**

# Careers in KM

*Unlike capital, knowledge is most valuable when it is controlled and used by those on the front lines of the organization.*

—C.A. Bartlett and S. Ghoshal, "Changing the Role of the Top Management: Beyond Systems to People," *Harvard Business Review*, May-June 1995, pp. 132–142.

*The dogmas of the quiet past are inadequate to the stormy present. The occasion is piled high with difficulty, and we must rise to the occasion. As our case is new, so we must think anew and act anew.*

—Abraham Lincoln

### Chapter Fourteen Learning Objectives

- ❑ Understand that the education and training of the KM workers works best when it is interdisciplinary in nature.
- ❑ Recognize the three categories that KM-related job titles typically fall into.
- ❑ Understand that the science/art of KM has fewer generally accepted principles and definitions than the management of physical or financial assets.
- ❑ Be aware of the rising demand for access to business knowledge has provided new career paths for knowledge workers.

The field of KM offers several choices for careers, and the practice of KM applies to any career. Few blessings in this world compare with the joy of spending your days working at a career you enjoy. As a public space for self-expression, nothing beats your career. What you choose to work at and how you pursue the goals of your career will determine not only how you will spend more than 50% of your waking hours, but also what value much of the world will see in you. Career choices are hugely important crossroads in our lives. Having a fulfilling career requires getting in touch with what is really important and then pursuing your goals relentlessly.

The education and training of KM workers works best when it is interdisciplinary in nature. Those pursuing a career in KM should be working to develop skills in a variety of areas. Try to learn as many industry-specific businesses and communication processes as possible. Pay special attention to the organization of intellectual assets, information needs analysis and inventories, methods of eliciting tacit knowledge, and the development of information standards, policies, and procedures. Typical KM-related job titles fall into three major categories: strategic, developmental, and tactical.

## Strategic KM Roles

Strategic KM positions include titles such as Chief Knowledge Officer or Chief Learning Officer. This is usually a visionary leader, possessing a thorough knowledge of the long-term strategic and competitive needs of the organization. Their role is to lead in the development of corporate culture, manage organizational change, and facilitate the creation and utilization of corporate knowledge management services. Persuasiveness, negotiation skills, and public speaking skills are critical in this role to define, develop, and distribute a global KM strategy.

It takes an extremely extroverted person to spend every workday establishing relationships to promote complex knowledge transfer between teams separated by time, distance, competition, and worldview. Although external leaders are sometimes brought in, they are often unsuccessful in this role because of the lack of strong personal contacts and earned trust (social capital) within the company. Typically, it is easier and cheaper to assign this task to someone who is already well respected and well experienced within the company.

## Developmental KM Roles

Individuals charged with the developmental tasks in a corporate KM program often have titles like Knowledge Engineer and Knowledge Architects. KM developers need excellent communication skills for gathering data and process-related information as well as the ability to build the necessary trust to achieve the tacit knowledge transfer. Valuable areas of knowledge include meeting facilitation, psychology, learning theory, library science, database development and administration, systems analysis, ERP integration, groupware development, XML, instant messaging, and peer-to-peer networking.

Conflict resolution skills are particularly valuable for knowledge engineers. As the individuals charged with integrating the people, processes, and technologies that support the organization, knowledge engineers must be able to gain the trust and cooperation of those whose jobs they are seeking to automate. Resistance to this process is to be expected, but not ignored. Don't assume that the input employees give you comes from a purely selfish point of view. Most workers honestly want to share their knowledge, but they fear that any knowledge they share will be ignored or (worse) misused. In discussions with fearful members of the status quo, try to focus on the new opportunities for strategic work that will be created by reducing their tactical responsibilities.

## Tactical

The third major KM role is the tactical role of Knowledge Researcher or Knowledge Worker. Their role is to search for, retrieve, document, and utilize valuable business knowledge. KM, at the tactical level, is the job of all knowledge workers. The best knowledge workers strive to constantly improve their investigation, research, learning, and analytical skills. They cultivate a diverse network of timely information resources, engaging dialogue forums and reciprocal relationships that allow them to raise their own level of expertise.

Team learning, collaboration, and knowledge management all represent different ways of providing a sustainable platform for future growth and innovation. The science/art of managing organizational knowledge-sharing strategies has far fewer generally accepted principles and definitions than the management of physical or financial assets. This causes confusion over the roles, responsibilities, and training required. Until these principles and definitions are clarified, KM will probably remain more of a discipline than a career field.

## The Playing Field

The rising demand for access to business knowledge has provided new career paths for knowledge workers. People who can gather and analyze, evaluate, summarize, and disseminate information in a useful manner are sure to have a bright future ahead of them, if they keep their skills current, their minds open, and their social network growing. Many schools of Library and Information Sciences are introducing classes and degrees that support a career in high-level KM positions and departments.

The Haas School of Business (Berkeley, CA), using a $1 million grant from Xerox and its Japanese affiliate, created a Chair of Knowledge and named Ikujiro Nonaka, Japanese management expert and author, as Berkeley's first Distinguished Professor of Knowledge. Kent State University's School of Library and Information Science offers a master's in Science in Knowledge Management. The University of Michigan Business School offers a doctorate with areas of study in knowledge management. As part of the growing trend, even Pepperdine University's Graziadio School of Business and Management included a KM component in its MBA program.

No individual discipline or group of people has a monopoly on knowledge. Knowledge is generated in dynamic ways through rapidly changing networks of human interaction, so in reality this makes any career a potential stepping stone into the KM field. Remember that the utility of a network is $N$ times the square of the nodes; Utility = $(Nodes)^2$. The effect of this rule is that small but ongoing increases in your personal network size, strength, and diversity can have an exponential impact on your potential for success.

KM practitioners believe that some environments support knowledge sharing and some inhibit it. The best practices for effective management of these environmental conditions in the future will be influenced and designed by the knowledge workers of today. By promoting a culture of openness, trust, learning, and dialogue, anyone can demonstrate thought leadership in the emerging field of KM. Individuals and organizations cannot avoid participating in knowledge-based competition, so it is clear that they must master it. To lead your company into this brave new world, start examining the following seven areas that apply to any business.

1. *Customer knowledge.* This is any company's most vital knowledge, according to every survey. Data mining, customer profiling, contact management, and intelligence processing are ways in which technology helps, but the real keys are active listening and shared memory. Constantly search your imagination and the world around you for new ways to use the customer knowledge you gain to add value for the customer.

2. *Industry and market knowledge.* Dynamic information connections, such as through the Internet, trade journals, competitive intelligence, and other systems, can give knowledge workers the foresight to plan industry changes. Recognizing the need for a new business model, six months before your competition, can make or break a company. Keep your information capture process fresh through constant incremental improvement.

3. *Process knowledge.* Documenting and propagating best practices are one way of converting human knowledge—gained the hard way: through experience—into explicit procedures and automated routines. Workflow tools allow you to build knowledge capture and knowledge sharing into your businesses processes. Knowledge leaders often use ERP projects and other high-visibility initiatives to get existing staff to think about their work in more explicit terms. This allows sharing a certain amount of documentation and other vital information behind the scenes, without the need for a commitment from all parties to some huge KM project.

4. *Knowledge exchange in products and services.* Smart knowledge workers can add value to their products and services with embedded intelligence. Some even use the data collected in the course of their operations to make their products more compelling and to encourage customer loyalty. For example, amazon.com has recently instituted a Corporate Accounts program. This program offers many advantages to corporations and institutional customers, such as:

- ❏ Multiple authorized purchasers can buy items for one corporate account, and account managers can track purchases across their organization.

- ❏ Corporate account customers are given the opportunity to apply for a credit account, which allows corporate purchasers to pay by purchase order and receive one detailed monthly bill for all corporate purchases.

- ❏ Account managers are able to log in to the corporate account management area to view all orders placed on the corporate account. Adding or deleting authorized buyers, and seeing what they are reading, can all be handled in one secure place.

By simply improving the ability of customers to see aggregated results of company purchases, amazon.com has provided a strong incentive for companies and customers to remain loyal to their brand. In the process of meeting their customers' needs, amazon revolutionized their entire business sector. Book selling will never be the same!

5. *People knowledge.* Expert systems, knowledgebases, and even company directories attempt to reinforce the all-important connections among the different parts of an organization. One of the tragedies of our times is that many of us have become our own secretaries, with far too little training. These systems help fill the vital role of enabling people to connect, communicate, and collaborate more effectively.

6. *Knowledge assets.* Intellectual capital is one of the key foundations of an information economy. A recent Columbia University study estimated that spending on intangible assets such as research and development and employee training results in returns that are eight times greater than an equal investment in new plants and equipment. New machinery only allows incremental improvements, whereas investment in intellectual capital can lead to revolutionary advances. Finding ways to account for and value these intangible assets is one of the key challenges confronting KM thought leaders today.

7. *Shared group memory.* Databases, document management, change control, and efficient information retrieval are common tools for managing organizational memory. Many organizations are now hiring corporate librarians to manage the mountains of shared memory that they have accumulated. Once they are properly managed, these assets can be reexamined, reused, and remembered to add tremendous strength to any organization. Look for compelling stories that promote your values, innovative processes that raise your profits, and best practices that keep your people safe.

As you can see from the previous list, no single leader is likely to be effective in leading change in this long list of areas. Cultural change, like knowledge creation itself, exists in the interactions between people. It is a social process that works best in an environment of mutually shared vision, interdependency, and trust.

## Preparing Yourself for Change

Our world today is in a state of constant change. To survive in this turmoil and to succeed requires different skills, mindset, and preparations than the jobs of the past. This book has introduced a large array of topics that affect you and the knowledge exchange happening around you. You must choose your path for the future and the level of drive that you apply to your career choice. Here is a short list of personal strategies to help you choose the right path.

### Top Ten Personal KM Strategies for the Future

1. *Share knowledge.* Whatever your expertise, giving some of it away will build your skills, credibility, social network, and self-esteem. Continually strive to give your job away, cross-train others, document your position, and build procedures and automation logic into your job. Be willing to take on more responsibility, document and assess your new

responsibility as quickly as possible, and meet with the person who gave you this responsibility to make sure that you both are working from a basis of shared understanding.

2. *Keep learning every day.* Some say that in the absence of new learning, today's engineering graduate is obsolete in less than five years. New learning comes from new challenges. So don't ask yourself why you should take on more responsibilities for the same compensation. Ask yourself why you should stay at a company if it does not offer you ample growth opportunities. The answer is—don't.

3. *Stick to your morals.* The interdependence of virtue and knowledge has been recognized since ancient times. With regard to virtue and knowledge, one invariably leads to another, and in the absence of one, the other will never develop.

4. *Be the master of your own fate.* When it comes to careers, in big companies or in small companies, you are essentially on your own. Through training, mentoring, and HR programs, companies may try to help, but they are subject to impersonal market conditions like stock price fluctuations, market changes, and international competition; so there are no guarantees. You have to take charge of your own destiny. No one is ever likely to care more about your career than you do.

5. *Find a job that you love!* People have very different goals and desires. This makes certain people better suited for certain kinds of careers. You have talents that fit you for some jobs and disqualify you from others. Take time for introspection; assess your skills, temperament, and talents and make your career decisions accordingly.

6. *Build your people skills.* It's better to be a people person with average skills (and the power of Metcalfe's Law) than to be an abrasive expert who wins at the expense of others. Because friends are your best allies in your life and in your career, no one will help you more than they will. Manage your contacts as if your career depends on them—because it usually does.

When building your social network, every person you meet is important. Make life a little easier for those around you, and you will build the type of trust, shared understanding, and shared commitment that you need to be successful. It has been apparent for some time that employers hire their friends first. When companies recruit from a group of outsiders, they interview, test, and screen heavily. Friendships can often allow you to bypass screening and move directly to negotiating your compensation.

7. *Don't sell yourself short.* Many new graduates make the mistake of assuming that they can start working for a company at well below market rates and then expect to see much better compensation after proving themselves. Typically, this does not work out. Companies have tons of procedures and policies to ensure that the compensation of existing workers does not grow too quickly. Starting for a company at a below-market rate only makes the problem worse.

In the IT field, this issue has led to what some are calling a loyalty crisis. High-tech workers have realized that they can expect a 3% to 10% annual raise for staying with their companies and a 25% to 60% raise for changing companies. This has resulted in a change from thinking about a career at a specific company to a career in the Information Technology field in general.

Unfortunately, jumping from job to job can have extremely unpredictable consequences. In a growing and expanding industry like Computer Science, job changing isn't necessarily a problem because there are always too few experienced workers. But in a declining industry such as oil and gas, established companies are downsizing and outsourcing. Some industries value the depth of experience that a long, stable career builds, whereas others look for the breadth of experience created by frequent job changes. The important thing is to know the preferences of your industry.

8. *Contribute something substantial and measurable every day.* Because you are only as good as your last success, attempt to keep a written record of your accomplishments. In this age of restructuring, managers are reporting that more and more of their time on the job is devoted to justifying their own existence and the existence of their department.

9. *Persevere relentlessly.* Don't let yourself be out of work, even for a day. Volunteer, work part time, or help a friend. Do something to interact with the world. Make contacts, observe carefully, and look for new opportunities. There are people all around you who need your help.

10. *You are NOT your job.* Too many people define themselves by their job title. If your career is your whole life, you're heading for disappointment and burnout. Highly successful people are the most subject to burnout. Don't stay in a job you hate. Hating your daily routine can ruin your health, and it can make everyone around you, including your spouse and family, miserable. Take a risk! Take action! Change things!

## Building a KM Resume

As mentioned earlier, KM careers are still being defined, but starting a career in KM right out of college is becoming more likely all of the time. If you are not able to begin in the KM career of your dreams, then begin by implementing KM techniques in the jobs that you do get and document the success on your resume. Build a resume based on the knowledge exchange that you created within the teams with which you worked. Give real-life examples of success and failures that show, regardless of the outcome, that you captured the relevant information, created dialogue, and documented what increased and reduced the success of the project.

### Getting the Job

Getting a job is typically based on education, experience, references, social skills, and appearance. KM cannot change the amount of education that you have to put on your resume, but it can help you organize your educational experience, help you learn and retain more information, and improve your ability to present that experience through your resume and orally during an interview. If nothing else, a KM perspective should have led you to build a network for yourself, and a strong social network is usually considered the most important factor for job seekers.

### Doing the Job

KM helps you harness your intelligence, knowledge, and wisdom for dissemination. Using dialogue to exchange information and foster knowledge creation will help you build relationships that can be used for references as well as social skills that help while interviewing. Experience and appearance are two things that we often think are beyond our control, yet how hard you work at these two items often makes a powerful statement during an interview. Lack of experience can be offset by hard work and enthusiasm; plain or poor features can be offset by posture, cleanliness, and neatness.

Knowledge exchange is happening. How will you harness it to better yourself and others? Begin with ethical behavior; do not focus your career on getting even when you are wronged. When others behave poorly, focus on the issues, and strive to maintain lines of communication. Being a peacemaker does not mean that you give in to wrong behavior, but it does include active listening and openmindedness to others' ideas. Seek to establish mutual understanding and mutually shared commitment before deciding that someone with an opposing point of view must be crazy.

Be willing to let projects and systems reach their end; don't try to continually breathe new life into an old idea, project, or system that has reached the end of its usefulness. Own the project; don't let the project own you. When you are responsible for ending someone else's project or system, recognize their need for closure and involve them as much as possible. Sometimes a good solution is to task the individual or team with documenting the project or team's past success and effectiveness. When shutting down a project or system, it is important to accomplish the following:

- ❑ Determine the reason for the project or system's end of life.
- ❑ Communicate to all parties the nature of the change.
- ❑ Involve project or system stakeholders in preparing documentation.
- ❑ Remember to respect the dignity of all individuals involved.

Change is difficult, but those who properly manage it will advance in their careers. Maintaining relationships, dignity, and ethics during change is a worthy goal for life.

### Keeping the Job

Once you get a job, don't be overwhelmed by the negative information moving through the office. Your company may be headed for layoffs, but that should not stop you from doing your job to the best of your abilities; however, be smart, don't let opportunities pass you by because you fear change.

## Company Strategies

In today's economy, companies are rewarded more often for growth than sustainability. Often, employees are hired into management positions without being given the authority to make real change. Would it not make better sense to automate the position than simply hiring an employee to be a robot? People make poor robots; humans need the ability to express their own creativity and to feel worthy in their jobs. The strategy of senior management can sometimes be summed up in two words: stock growth. Stock options inspire executives to pursue stock growth in a company, not necessarily sustainable growth of the business. The dot.com companies of the late 1990s were built on a business model focused solely on stock growth, not sustainable dividends, but short-term share price growth. It was like athletes taking steroids for maximum short-term performance, even though it shortens their lives.

One strategy that senior management uses to show the analysts that they are serious about growth is to merge with or take over a competitor. These transitions invariably create winners and losers. No matter what the direction of your company, skills in managing the exchange of knowledge are more likely to make you come out a winner than the tired old strategy of knowledge hoarding.

## Where Is the Knowledge Exchange?

One way to determine a business's direction is looking for the knowledge exchange. If the company is concerned about sustainable growth, it will build knowledge exchange into its growth strategy. Would it be wise to spend millions or billions on acquiring your competitor without determining what knowledge and information they had? If you buy a company in the Information Age without building a method for off-loading or integrating their information, knowledge, and wisdom, what have you bought?

If a company is purchasing or merging with other companies without building in knowledge exchange, how will they sustain their growth and ROI? If you are working for a company that is not sharing their direction, building knowledge exchanges, or valuing the knowledge and wisdom of their employees, it is unlikely you will ever retire from that company.

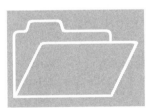

### Final Case Study: Railroad Watches

During the 1920s, two companies, the Illinois Watch Company and the Hamilton Watch Company, dominated the market for precision railroad watches. The Illinois Watch Company's premier watch was the Bunn Special, and it outperformed everything that the Hamilton Watch Company had, in both accuracy and durability. The executives at the Hamilton Watch Company realized that they could not close the technology gap quickly enough to continue to compete, so in 1927 they bought their competitor.

The purchase was made to gain control of the market and to integrate the Illinois Watch Company's superior watch design into the Hamilton Watch Company's products. Hamilton made this purchase because of the skill and knowledge of the Illinois's employees, not because it was trying to impress investors or stock analysts. The result was that Hamilton's premier watches, an example being the 992B, came to be seen as one of the world's most accurate and reliable railroad watches.

The buyout of the Illinois Watch Company and the integration of their technology enabled the Hamilton Watch Company to dominate this highly technical field for more than 30 years. To this day, collectors all over the world admire the watches they created.

## Conclusion

Effective knowledge management and collaborative learning techniques offer companies and their employees their best chance of sustaining success in today's high-tech, networked, just-in-time market. KM is social, and to some extent is a part of all jobs.

In this text, we have introduced you to a wide range of KM tools, techniques, and terminology for enhancing innovation, communication, and dedication among individuals and workgroups. The chapters have covered a wide range of existing KM thought leadership and have focused on real-world business examples using commonly available technologies.

Effective KM requires a set of conceptual tools that enable us to navigate complex issues within a framework of networked social relationships. Recognizing and adapting to the changing pace and rules of our networked economy calls for new skills and new ways of thinking. The rigorous modeling methods, disciplined information management techniques, and intelligent use of social capital taught in this text provide the practical tools that will lead to new levels of business agility and success.

This is your beginning. In completing this book, you have been made aware of the knowledge exchange research that is happening around you. To become peers, you simply have to collaborate and add to that body of knowledge and research. In the future, we will look forward to working with you and sharing what you learn about knowledge management in business.

### Additional Learning Resources

❑ *The Reflective Practitioner: How Professionals Think in Action*, by Donald A. Schon (1983)

❑ www.dom.edu/gslis/ckmmasters.html—Dominican University (River Forest, IL) Master of Science in Knowledge Management

❑ http://jiju.gmu.edu/catalog/spp/spp_nps2.html—George Mason University (Fairfax, VA) Master of Science in New Professional Studies in Knowledge Management

❑ www.royalroads.ca/channels/for+learners/divisions+and+schools/science+ technology+and+environment/diplomas+and+certificates/graduate+diploma+ in+km.htm—Royal Roads University (Victoria, British Columbia) Graduate Diploma in Knowledge Management

❑ www.ou.edu/cas/slis/news/mskm.htm—University of Oklahoma (Tulsa and Norman, OK) Master of Science in Knowledge Management

❑ http://dept.kent.edu/rags-alpha/catalog/IAKM/pdf—Kent State University (Kent, OH) Master of Science in Information Architecture and Knowledge Management

 **Test Your Knowledge**

## Discussion Questions

1.  How flexible are your career plans?

2.  Do you have goals set for your future?

3.  Are you meeting your current goals?

4.  Do you have a career mentor?

## Review Questions

1.  What you choose to work at and how you pursue the goals of your career will determine not only how you will spend more than _____% of your waking hours, but also what value much of the _____ will see in you.

2.  Strategic KM positions include titles such as _____ or Chief Learning Officer.

3.  KM developers need excellent _____ skills for gathering data and process-related information as well as the ability to build the necessary trust to achieve the tacit knowledge transfer.

4.  The third major KM role is the _____ role of Knowledge Researcher or Knowledge Worker.

5.  Knowledge is generated in _____ ways through rapidly changing networks of human interaction.

6.  As mentioned earlier, KM careers are still being defined, but starting a career in KM right out of college is becoming more _____ all of the time.

7. KM cannot change the amount of _____ that you have to put on your resume, but it can help you organize your educational experience, help you learn and retain more information, and improve your ability to present that experience through your resume and _____ during an interview.

8. KM helps you _____ your intelligence, knowledge, and wisdom for dissemination.

9. When others behave poorly, focus on the issues, and strive to maintain lines of _____.

10. Be willing to let projects and systems reach their end; don't try to continually _____ new life into an old idea, project, or system that has reached the end of its usefulness.

11. In today's economy, companies are rewarded more often for growth than _____.

12. No matter what the direction of your company, _____ in managing the exchange of knowledge are more likely to make you come out a _____ than the tired old strategy of knowledge hoarding.

13. If a company is purchasing or merging with other companies without building in _____ _____, how will they sustain their growth and ROI?

14. KM is _____, and to some extent is a part of all jobs.

15. Effective KM requires a set of conceptual _____ that enable us to _____ complex issues within a framework of networked social relationships.

# Index

Page references followed by "f" denote figures; those followed by "t" denote tables.